Black
FORTUNES

Black
Fortunes

THE STORY OF THE FIRST SIX AFRICAN
AMERICANS WHO ESCAPED SLAVERY
AND BECAME MILLIONAIRES

SHOMARI WILLS

Amistad

An Imprint of HarperCollins*Publishers*

BLACK FORTUNES. Copyright © 2018 by Shomari Wills. All rights reserved. Printed in the United States of America. No part of this book may be used or reproduced in any manner whatsoever without written permission except in the case of brief quotations embodied in critical articles and reviews. For information, address HarperCollins Publishers, 195 Broadway, New York, NY 10007.

HarperCollins books may be purchased for educational, business, or sales promotional use. For information, please email the Special Markets Department at SPsales@harpercollins.com.

FIRST EDITION

Designed by Renata De Oliveira

Library of Congress Cataloging-in-Publication Data has been applied for.

ISBN 978-0-06-243759-4

18 19 20 21 22   LSC   10 9 8 7 6 5 4 3 2 1

*To the decendents of those who came to
this country in bondage and persevered to
reveal our true greatness.*

*In particular, to my wife, Aprielle,
my daughter, Zora, and my entire family*

Contents

Introduction

I grew up hearing stories from my mother about "Uncle Johnnie" the millionaire. My great-great-uncle John Mott Drew, born in 1883, was a boisterous man with a hearty laugh who dressed in all-black three-piece suits and wore a white Panama hat on top of a head of wavy white hair. He was known for being frugal despite his wealth and gave the children in the family two-dollar bills and silver dollars for Christmas.

Before he rose to millionaire status, John Drew was the son of a slave. His father, Napoleon Bonaparte Drew, was enslaved on a large plantation called Belmead in Powhatan, Virginia. Napoleon had a zealous work ethic and an innate sense of self-confidence, which he passed down to his children. After Emancipation, he bought a farm in 1897 near the plantation where he had been enslaved and became the first black person in Powhatan County to own property. In 1875, he rented out his farmland and Napoleon moved north to Darby, Pennsylvania, a suburb of Philadelphia, with his wife, three sons, and a daughter. When his children reached adult-hood, Napoleon sold most of the land in Powhatan. "Take the money from my land and make something of yourselves," he told his children. In 1901, Simon Drew, his eldest son, opened an "ice-house" in Darby where he sold oysters, beer, and ice cream. Simon was known for the parties he threw at his restaurant as well as for being a look-alike for Frederick Douglass, with long white hair smoothed back tightly and a distinguished beard. After opening a restaurant, he bought four apartment build-ings in the black suburbs of Philadelphia and became a landlord.

His brother John Mott Drew was an even shrewder investor. John started his career in real estate like Simon, but he eventually branched out to other, more lucra-tive businesses. In 1919, he noticed that the people in the majority-black towns of Yeadon and Darby, where he also lived, had no way to get to work in Philadelphia and nearby Lansdowne, Pennsylvania. He took matters into his own hands, bought a bus, and began driving a jitney route from the suburbs to the cities. When he founded the John Drew Bus Line, he became the first African American to own a bus line. The enterprise grew over time, adding six buses to its fleet and several dozen employees. In 1930, he sold his business to a larger conglomerate under the condition that it would retain his black employees and never allow segregation on his bus route.

John Drew was also a stock trader. He knew that di-rectly trading stocks himself would prove extremely difficult, and hired a white broker to trade secretly on his behalf. During the Roaring Twenties, John invested the profits from his bus company sale into the stock market and benefited from the historically profitable bull market. In the late 1920s, sensing that the roaring stock market had entered a bubble, he told his broker to pull his money out. He walked away with over $250,000 ($3.5 million)* just months before many other investors were wiped out by the Great Crash of 1929.

John purchased a local Negro League baseball team, the Darby Daisies. He operated the team for two years, until it folded in 1932 due to low attendance, as during the Great Depression fans had less money for recreational activities. John turned the ballpark into a "gentleman's farm," furnishing it with livestock that grazed on the infield. John died without a will. His story made me realize that the economic achievement of African Americans dates further back than today's black elite.

The creation of black wealth is an important but overlooked subject in the economic and social history of the United States. African Americans were treated as property during slavery and were stripped of their economic and social personhood—reduced to commodities to be controlled, managed, bought, sold, underwritten, and leveraged. Attaining economic independence and power was a revolutionary act.

Black millionaires disrupt stereotypes of black economic impotence. They remind us that African

---

* Throughout, all amounts in parentheses represent figures in today's dollars.

Americans do not lack the desire or ability to work or build businesses and wealth, but that instead they have often had to overcome great struggles to achieve economic stability, let alone independence and power.

Early in our county's history, African Americans who achieved wealth were often attacked, demonized, or swindled out of their money by those who knew the Jim Crow court system would offer no redress to a black person. The black elite in their first decades of existence survived assassination attempts, lynchings, frivolous lawsuits, and criminal cases all meant to destroy or delegitimize their wealth. Madam C. J. Walker was memorialized as the first black millionaire not because she was the first to achieve wealth—she was far from the first—but because she was one of the first African Americans to flaunt and claim her wealth openly and fearlessly. The earliest black millionaires were conditioned not to be so brazen.

Black Fortunes tells the story of Mary Ellen Pleasant, Robert Reed Church, O. W. Gurley, Hannah Elias, Annie Turnbo Malone, and Madam C. J. Walker, America's first cohort of black millionaires, and their journey to liberty and wealth.

Mary Ellen Pleasant's story begins in the 1820s and spans nearly a century. She was a free black woman who was raised in New England during the whaling boom of the 1830s and 1840s that inspired Herman Melville's most famous work, *Moby-Dick*. She left New England for California during the gold rush of 1849 and became wealthy as a commodity trader, a moneylender, and the proprietress of high-end boarding-houses. She used her wealth to fund John Brown's raid on Harpers Ferry and supported suffrage and civil rights activists and causes.

Robert Reed Church was born a plantation slave during the peak of the cotton trade, the product of a liaison between a wealthy white steamboat captain and his black concubine. He escaped slavery during the Civil War and became one of the largest landowners in Memphis.

Annie Malone was the daughter of slaves. She was abandoned at an early age and raised by her sister in Illinois. As a young woman, she invented a number of black hair products, which she later built into America's largest hair brand.

At the turn of the century, O. W. Gurley, a school-teacher from Pine Bluff, Arkansas, built an all-black neighborhood in Tulsa, Oklahoma, called Greenwood, which became known as "Black Wall Street." The enclave served as a refuge for African Americans seeking a middle-class life and a safe haven from the lynchings and racial violence of the South, until it was destroyed by a white mob in 1921 during the Tulsa race riots.

Hannah Elias was the black mistress of a white New York millionaire who heaped money on her. She used his gifts to decorate her mansion to look like Cleopatra's palace. When her wealth and affair with a white man were revealed, angry mobs set upon her house, and she was arrested. Elias eventually beat the charges and moved to Harlem, where she helped John Nail, a black real estate developer, turn the neighborhood into an enclave for New York's black residents.

Researching the stories of these titans of industry was challenging, because they died more than one hundred years ago (with the exception of Annie Malone, who passed away in 1956). Few records exist concerning African Americans before 1865. At the time, they were often viewed as noncitizens and seldom cataloged by census takers or vital-records keepers. Further, in many cases, these men and women were self-educated and could read but not write effectively, and as a result they did not keep diaries or engage in letter writing. They had small families and only a few of their children lived to adulthood, leaving virtually no surviving relatives to tell their stories directly. Therefore, I relied on extensive archival research. I painted the stories of these accomplished people by surveying their own writings and letters, newspaper clippings, and oral accounts by their contemporaries that were documented. I labored over any available vital records. In hundreds of hours of research, I have given an earnest effort to deliver an accurate and fair portrayal of these individuals' lives and their work.

The establishment of wealth is fundamental to social and political progress. Wealth has the ability to transform communities and close gaps in racial disparities. During these individuals' lives, which span the nineteenth and early twentieth centuries, an era when African Americans needed housing, jobs, and funding for political campaigns and activism, it was the black wealthy class that often supplied the means. Many successful black Americans, including the luminaries of *Black Fortunes* and my great-great-uncle John Drew, had to use white proxies to perform financial transactions to avoid being excluded on the basis of race.

Today, as Oprah Winfrey, Michael Jordan, and Robert Smith make up the first cohort of black billionaires, it's important not to lose sight of the history and battles that were waged and are still being fought to make such achievement possible.

These stories are a neglected part of not only black history but also American history, and they deserve to be told and woven into the tapestry of our shared history. Through the stories of America's first black millionaires, we see the limitless potential of black Americans despite structural inequalities, and we can glimpse the hope for one day achieving racial economic parity.

Black
FORTUNES

Prologue:
The First Black Millionaire

On a warm night in 1841, William Alexander Leidesdorff sat on the porch of an old white house covered in vines in New Orleans with his fiancée, Hortense. As she leaned on Leidesdorff, she could tell that something was bothering him. Hortense looked into his heavy-lidded, auburn eyes. "What is troubling you, William?" she asked, looking up at him with her big blue eyes framed by blond curls. Against his better judgment, he confided in her.

He stammered as he tried to get the words out. "I'm a . . ." He finally told her. Hortense's eyes filled with tears.

As she took in his confession, she scanned his features. He had a round, pale face with a straight nose, ruddy cheeks, piercing deep-set brown eyes, bushy sideburns, and curly brown hair that he wore slicked back with oil. As he cried, he confessed that he was from the Virgin Islands, the son of a Jewish Danish sailor and merchant and a black island woman. He had been passing for white since he had arrived in New Orleans from the Caribbean as a boy, rising from working on the docks to commanding a ship in his midtwenties. Hortense plunged her face into the sleeve of his velvet jacket and sobbed heavily. "My father will never let us marry, and I cannot deceive or disobey him." "Our dream has ended, but I will love you as long as I live," he said.

"Go! You must go," Hortense told Leidesdorff. "My heart will always belong to you. Run, William! I must tell my father!" she shouted after him as he retreated into the night.

Hortense came from an aristocratic New Orleans family that owned slaves and would strongly disapprove of Hortense marrying a man of color. After Leidesdorff left, she went inside the house and told her father about him. Incensed, her father announced that the wedding was off, dragged her to the door of her room, and pushed her inside. "You will never see that nigger again," he swore, turning the key and locking her in.

The next day, Leidesdorff received a package from Hortense's father with the engagement ring inside and decided to leave New Orleans. He sold everything he owned and purchased a ship. The day before he was to leave the city, he was walking down Canal Street, and was passed by a funeral procession. He stood in the doorway of a store and watched the mourners go by. He spotted Hortense's mother, father, and sister in one of the carriages, and his heart sank. That night there was a knock at the door. When he opened it he was greeted by a priest. The man handed Leidesdorff a small gold cross, which he immediately recognized as Hortense's. "Hortense's last words were that she wanted you to have this," the priest told him.

In 1841, Leidesdorff left New Orleans. He sailed to California, then a remote Mexican territory. As he stepped off the gangplank of his ship in Yerba Buena Cove, he saw a backwater of thick forest and green hills dotted with Indian communities, military forts, cattle farms, and Catholic missions. Deciding he would live openly as a mixed-race man, he settled in San Francisco and started an import-export company shipping tallow and animal pelts from California to Hawaii and Alaska. Once that business turned a profit, he used the money to open a general store, a warehouse, a lumberyard, and a shipbuilding business; he also built San Francisco's first hotel. San Francisco had very few inhabitants at the time. Leidesdorff, still trying to mend his broken heart, seemed to relish the isolation. His only friends were his employees, a bartender at his hotel, and his black laundress. At night they would go down to the beach on the northern coast of San Francisco to swim. Sometimes they'd just sit on the rocks, looking up at the moon, and talk until the sun came up, listening to the waves crash on the shore.

In 1844, Leidesdorff, then Mexican California's most prominent resident, was granted citizenship by the Mexican government. In return for his allegiance,

Mexico gave him more than 35,000 acres of undeveloped land. His acquisition made him the largest landowner in the area.

Leidesdorff built a large mansion in the hills of San Francisco, which he referred to with tongue in cheek as "the cottage." His house was a New Orleans–style home with dozens of rooms, a wraparound porch, and the state's only flower garden. His estate functioned as a de facto US embassy in Mexican California territory. A convivial host, he received generals and politicians at his residence. He served his guests beer and meat and offered them cigars. He apologized for not having better whiskey, which was hard to come by in the West. "We get what we can get," he would tell them. "Would you like some tequila?" He spoke with a strange accent, a mix of his father's Danish, his mother's Caribbean patois, and a southern drawl.

In 1846, when Mexico went to war with the United States, Leidesdorff switched his allegiance to the Americans and was appointed United States Vice Consul to Mexico. After the Mexican–American War ended and the US annexed California, the US government made Leidesdorff the treasurer of the territory. In 1847, he built California's first public school and a horse racing track for the citizens' entertainment. In 1848, when gold was discovered in the Sacramento valley, the value of his property and business skyrocketed to over $1 million, making him the first African American to achieve a net worth of more than a million dollars in the history of the United States.

One spring night, Leidesdorff retired to bed in his quarters on the top floor of his mansion. The next morning, doctors pronounced him dead of "brain fever." Flags in San Francisco were hung at half-mast, and Californians wept for the loss of one of their most beloved.

After his death, Joseph Folsom, a real estate investor, traveled to the Virgin Islands and found Leidesdorff's estranged mother, Anna Marie Sparks, his sole known heir. He convinced her to sign over her son's property for a payment of $75,000 ($2.1 million). The Leidesdorff estate was worth more than $1.4 million ($38 million). With the stroke of a pen, the fortune and legacy of America's first black millionaire was stolen.

This is a world of compensations.
—ABRAHAM LINCOLN, 1859

1

Abolitionism and Capitalism

~~~

August 12, 1841

NANTUCKET

The sun was warm, and the air smelled of the salt water on the sandy coast of Nantucket on August 12, 1841. On a dirt road lined with trees and hedges, in a library known as the Nantucket Atheneum, the town's first abolitionist convention came to order. Five hundred men and women took their seats, most of them local Quakers, the men in plain dark-colored suits with broad hats, the women in gray or brown dresses with bonnets. The Atheneum had once been a church and retained an exterior of white wood and stone with stained-glass windows and two stone columns at its entrance. Inside was a great room filled with benches of carved wood, bookshelves, and oil paintings on the wall. From a platform in the back, William C. Coffin, a local abolitionist, made an announcement: there was a fugitive slave in attendance, and he was going to give a speech.

Heads swiveled as Frederick Douglass stood and made his way toward the stage. He was tall with a muscular frame that showed through his shirt and vest, a square jaw, and a clean-shaven face, his hair coiled dark and parted and pushed across his forehead and down toward his ears. As he moved to the front of the room, members of the audience could see that he was shaking from stage fright.

Douglass, who was twenty-three years old, had escaped from slavery in Maryland three years earlier. He now lived in New Bedford, Massachusetts, and worked at a brass foundry. He was a preacher at the African Methodist Episcopal Zion church in his town, but had never spoken to an audience of more than a few dozen, nor had he much experience speaking in front of white people.

Douglass had come to Nantucket for a working vacation, hoping to stay abreast of the goings-on in the abolitionist struggle but more to relax on the island looking out on to the Atlantic Ocean. "Needing a day or two of rest, I attended this convention, never supposing that I should take part in the proceedings," he recalled. "Until now, I had taken no holiday since my escape from slavery." When Coffin asked him to come to the stage, he was so overcome with fear that he could barely keep his feet underneath him. As he took the stage, he felt ill. He summoned all his willpower to keep his back straight and his limbs steady, and then he began.

His voice trembled as he spoke of being born and raised on a slave plantation in Maryland. He stuttered as he described enduring backbreaking labor and brutality at the hands of overseers. The audience hung on his every word. One of the attendees recalled, "Flinty hearts were pierced, and cold ones melted by his eloquence. Our best pleaders for the slave held their breath for fear of interrupting him."

When Douglass finished, the well-known abolitionist William Lloyd Garrison, a slim man with thinning hair, leaped onto center stage. He praised Douglass and sermonized on the evils of slavery, whipping the crowd into a fury. "Have we been listening to a thing, a piece of property, or a man?" he demanded, motioning toward Douglass.

"A man!" the audience cried back in unison. "A man!"

"Shall such a man be held a slave in a Christian land?" Garrison demanded.

"No! No!" the audience shouted back, seeming to make the rafters shake. Douglass himself, moved by Garrison, recalled, "For a moment . . . a public meeting is transformed, as it were, into a single individuality— the orator wielding a thousand heads and hearts at once, and by the simple majesty of his all controlling thought, converting his hearers into the express image of his own soul."

The crowd was at a fever pitch, and Garrison continued, raising his voice, "Shall such a man ever be sent back to bondage from the free soil of old Massachusetts?" He motioned toward Douglass again.

"No! No! No!" the audience jumped to their feet and shouted. The noise poured out of the building and could be heard in the streets.

Afterward, as the convention let out, a crowd of men and women formed around Douglass who were eager to shake his hand, thump him on the back, and compliment him on his speech. When the crowd finally dissipated, a group of Nantucket's prominent black citizens, led by Edward J. Pompey, a free black whaler, industrialist, and ship commander, approached Douglass, brimming with pride. The group was from Newtown, Nantucket's black district, where Douglass was lodging. They escorted him out of the church and down a road past a fence that segregated Newtown from the rest of the town.

The walk from the Atheneum to Newtown took fifteen minutes as the group walked south, passing first the rest of town, then a cow pasture, and finally a fence made of wood planks. Above Newtown was a set of large windmills and, to the south, a settlement of displaced Wampanoag Indians who lived in the wilderness on the island's coast. Newtown was a cluster of houses erected along a grid of eleven streets; prominent among them was Angola Street, an allusion to the residents' African heritage. The center of the enclave was the African Meeting House, a square building with a gable roof, gray wood siding, and a wood-plank fence surrounding it. The African Meeting House was where Nantucket's black residents attended church and school, and on occasion it hosted African American visitors such as Douglass.

That night Douglass stayed up talking with the island's black residents, who also included the wealthy black whaling captain Absalom Boston and the leading black families of the island.

When morning came, Douglass left Newtown to attend the second day of the convention at the Atheneum. Excitement about his speech seemed to have grown overnight, and when he entered the hall, people crowded around him, thumped his back, and showered him with adulation. The next day, he returned to mainland Massachusetts, where William Lloyd Garrison offered him a job as a traveling speaker for the Massachusetts Anti-Slavery Society. "I doubt anyone would want to hear me speak," Douglass told Garrison. Nonetheless, he accepted the offer and began traveling the country telling his story as he had in Nantucket. In the following months, Douglass rose to fame as an abolitionist and orator. His time on the island catapulted him to prominence and also galvanized the African American community there. Among them was a young woman who would become one of America's most powerful black entrepreneurs: Mary Ellen Pleasant.

~

IN 1814, IN AN APARTMENT IN A THREE-STORY BRICK BUILDING ON a stone street near Philadelphia's docks, Mary Ellen Williams entered the world. She was born free and black. Her parents christened her Mary Ellen Williams, taking her mother's first name and her father's last name. "My parents were a strange mixture. My father was a native Kanaka and my mother a full-blooded Louisiana negress," she recalled. Pleasant had her mother's brown skin and wavy hair and her father's tall stature and Polynesian features. Her father, a silk merchant named Louis Alexander Williams, was larger than life in her memory: "He was a man of great intelligence. He was like most of his race, a giant." Her mother did not leave a lasting impression on her. "I was named after my mother, but I really recall little else about her," Pleasant said.

Pleasant's time with her parents in their apartment was brief. They sent her to live on the island of Nantucket when she was seven years old to attend school. Like many free states, Pennsylvania was both antislavery and anti-integration. Black children, like Pleasant, were not welcome in Philadelphia's schools. In most free states during the antebellum era, there were no schooling options for African American children. In Nantucket and Cincinnati, private "colored schools" had been established where parents and sponsors could buy education for black children. In 1826, Williams took Pleasant on a steamship to live with associates of his, an island family called the Husseys, while she attended school on the Massachusetts island.

The Husseys were one of Nantucket's best-known and most powerful families. Members of their clan had controlling interests in most of the town's institutions, including the Religious Society of Friends (the formal name for the Quaker church) and local government and industry. They owned several houses and businesses spread across the island. Williams, a traveling fabric merchant, likely knew them as business associates. If he had known the Husseys more intimately, he perhaps would have known that they had a reputation for being dishonest. An old Nantucket verse described the Husseys: "The Rays and Russells coopers are / The knowing Folgers lazy / A lying Coleman very rare / And scarce an honest Hussey."

When Pleasant arrived on Nantucket, she was put into the care of Mary Hussey, an elderly Quaker woman who dressed in bonnets and long skirts. "Call me Grandma Hussey," she told Pleasant. Grandma Hussey ran a store in a wood building located beneath a grassy hill by the town's pier, a stone's throw away from the Atheneum. From the window, one could see sailors and merchants working away on ships and moving about drums of whale oil. After Williams left Pleasant in the Husseys' care, Grandma Hussey decided not to send Pleasant to school and instead made her work in her store. "My father, as I afterward learned, sent money every year for my education, but as I was an unusually smart girl and quick at everything, they kept me at work in the store."

Pleasant resented being kept out of school, but it was an early lesson about power dynamics in the antebellum era. "I envy children who can write a good hand

and spell correctly, and blame the Husseys for not giving me an education," she later said. The Husseys were
rich and white, and although Pleasant was privileged
to have been born free, the color of her skin and her
gender still allowed her to be taken advantage of. Thus
she came to better understand the world she lived in.
Either she could fight against those who had power, or
she could work with them and accept the limitations
that race and gender imposed upon her. She decided
to do both.

She ingratiated herself with the Husseys, making
herself indispensable in their store. As a girl, she foraged
the woods around the store for pokeberries, which she
would mash and strain to make a dark purple ink for
Grandma Hussey to sell. She learned to keep the books,
sweep and clean the store, and sell to customers. "I was
always on the watch, and few people could get out of the
store without buying something from me." She learned
to read and write in her spare time and used her work in
the store to learn about business and human behavior.
"I have let books alone and studied men and women a
great deal," she said. "You can't learn all the book knowledge and all the human nature studied in a lifetime.
You must slight one or the other." So she slighted books
and studied capital both human and financial.

During her years with the Husseys on Nantucket,
Pleasant nursed a resentment of racism and slavery.
When she wasn't working, she would venture south of
Grandma Hussey's shop through town, past the Newtown
fence, to enter Nantucket's free black community.

The inhabitants of Newtown were made up of black whalers, escaped slaves, and domestic servants. They were led by the town's most prominent citizen, Absalom Boston. Absalom was a well-muscled man with a beard that stretched from his ears down his entire jaw with no mustache. He wore gold hoop earrings, and his hair was coarse and pushed back into a pompadour. Absalom was black royalty in Nantucket. He was a descendant of the island's Indian natives and black slaves. His family was credited with having ended slavery on the island after his uncle Prince Boston had challenged the legality of slavery in Nantucket, sued for his freedom, and won.

Absalom inherited money from his parents, who died when he was young, and used it to build one of the first structures in Newtown, a small shop in a clapboard house, where he sold fishing equipment and groceries. In 1822, he bought and captained his own whaling ship called *Industry*, becoming the first black man in New England to own and lead a whaling outfit. Subsequently, he used his earnings to develop Newtown by underwriting mortgages for the houses of free blacks. Along with Boston and other prominent black Nantucketers, Pleasant attended church and learned about abolition before venturing back to her employer on the white side of the fence.

WHILE SHE WAS LEARNING ABOUT BLACK CULTURE AND THE LIB-eration struggle in Newtown, Pleasant bore witness to an economic transformation from the Husseys' shop by the harbor. From the shop, she could see oil refineries being built and whaling ships carrying whale carcasses and barrels of blubber. The Nantucket whaling boom was just getting under way when she arrived as a girl.

In the early nineteenth century, whale oil, used as lighting and heating oil, was rapidly becoming the United States' most prized commodity, second only to cotton, making whaling a highly profitable business. Nantucket, with its location in the Atlantic Ocean and its tradition of deep ocean fishing, was well positioned to hunt whales. As the demand for the oil increased, Nantucket's deep ocean fishing boats were refitted as whaling ships, and the town emerged as the largest producer of whale oil in the United States.

Before whale oil became readily available, most of the Western world lived in darkness once the sun went down. Candles and lamps fueled by cow and sheep fat were hard to produce, burned dimly, and gave off a foul odor. Whale oil, by contrast, burned brightly and was odorless. As it became broadly available in the United States and England, whaling exploded into an $11-million-a-year ($309 million) industry, becoming the third-largest economic sector in the United States after cotton and manufacturing. The boom made Nantucket one of the richest and busiest towns in the world during the years Pleasant was reared there.

Whaling was also a catalyst for social change. With the onset of whaling in Nantucket, men abandoned work in town for high-wage jobs working on docks and in open waters in whaling crews. In their absence, women became entrepreneurs and laborers, running the restaurants, stores, and hotels in town.

The whaling boom also created a black middle and upper class in Nantucket. Benefiting from racial stereotypes about their unnatural strength, black men were recruited to the island to hunt whales. Whaling offered a much better life than slave labor or tenement farming; in addition, men who worked on whaling crews were often shareholders, not employees, and were entitled to a percentage of the profits from the whales they helped bring in. As a result, black men in Nantucket could achieve moderate to high incomes that were unheard-of by blacks in the slave era. As the whaling industry grew, so did the black middle class on the island. Pleasant watched as Newtown grew from a poor village into an enclave of black middle-class families.

As a result of the emergence of the whaling industry, Pleasant was raised in a boomtown. She watched as people flocked to Nantucket to work on whaling ships, to open oil refineries or hotels and saloons to cater to the growing population. Some people made fortunes in Nantucket; others lost them. The lessons she learned from witnessing the boom would one day prove themselves useful.

IN THE DAYS FOLLOWING THE ABOLITIONIST CONVENTION AND Frederick Douglass's debut in 1841, Pleasant planned to make a move of her own. Not long after Douglass went back to Springfield, Massachusetts, she boarded a steamship for mainland Massachusetts at the Nantucket pier. "I went to Boston to better my condition," she later said.

Pleasant arrived in Boston around the year 1842, when she was twenty-six years old and got a job as an apprentice to a cobbler in a shop in Boston's South End. The South End was home to the city's monied class, men who wore broadcloth suits with gold watch chains hanging from their waistcoat pockets. Its streets were made of gravel and cobblestones and lined with baroque Victorian homes and mansions. At the shop, Pleasant learned to make boots and sew vests.

Pleasant hadn't left Nantucket to escape the Husseys or to find a better job or trade. On the contrary, she remained close with the Husseys and couldn't have hoped to provide a future for herself in shoemaking or any other trade she could learn. To secure a good life, a woman was expected to get married. To better her position, she needed to find a husband, and Boston's tony South End was as good a place as any to find a well-heeled one.

Pleasant was a striking woman. She was tall and slender with skin the color of clay, a long straight nose, high cheekbones, intense dark eyes, and long hair that was black and oiled straight. Perhaps her best feature was her charm and her way with words. "I have always noticed that when I have something to say people listen," she remarked. "They never go to sleep on me."

One day, James W. Smith, a well-dressed middle-aged businessman, entered the shop where she worked to do some shopping. He caught Pleasant's eye as she was doing her work. "I made sure to strike up a conversation with him before he left," she remembered. Smith didn't say much about himself, but he did say he was Cuban. Identifying as Hispanic awarded him a racial ambiguity that allowed him to better navigate the United States' racial caste system. The proportions of Spanish, Taino Indian, and African blood he possessed were simply left to the imagination, allowing him to avoid being classified as colored even under the strictest interpretation of the "one-drop rule." Pleasant did discover a bit of information about Smith: she learned that he was an abolitionist.

Pleasant had her sights locked on Smith after that day she met him in the shop. He was well off, and he shared her passion for racial justice. Pleasant, however, didn't make her interest in him obvious right away. She learned that he was a member of the Catholic church near her workplace, St. Mary's Church. Pleasant had grown up attending an African Methodist Episcopal Church in Nantucket but became Catholic to join Smith's congregation. "One church was the same as another to me," she later said. After joining St. Mary's, she became a member of the choir. The choir was positioned in the front of the church in full view of the congregation during service.

One night inside a steepled building made of rough stone on the north side of Boston, Smith finally took notice of the young woman he met in the store and at church. After Mass was over, Smith asked the priest, Father Trainor, to introduce him to Pleasant. Pleasant was brought to him, and he offered to walk her home.

As he walked her home that night under the moonlight, to Smith, it seemed they had been brought together by providence. He strolled with her unaware that Pleasant had set the forces that would bring them together into motion weeks before. A few days later, thoroughly charmed by Pleasant, he asked for her hand in marriage. "We were married inside of a month," she bragged.

AS NEWLYWEDS, MR. JAMES W. SMITH AND MRS. MARY ELLEN SMITH split time between his home in Boston and Smith's plantation in Charles Town, West Virginia. In Boston, Mary Ellen and James Smith entertained abolitionists together like William Lloyd Garrison, Wendell Phillips, Geo Green, and Louis Hayden.

In Charles Town, they spent time at Smith's mansion. The town was made up of Victorian homes and plantations built into the foothills of the Appalachian Mountains, looking down onto the Shenandoah River. It was picturesque, canopied by maple, cherry, pine, sycamore, and fruit trees and surrounded by green hills. Its estates spanned hundreds of acres with two- and three-story homes made of stone, barns and servants' quarters, tanneries, orchards, and acres of crop fields.

Smith's land was managed by a young African American man named John James Pleasants.*

There weren't many slaves in Charles Town, only a few hundred domestic servants and enslaved black miners. Salt mining drove West Virginia's economy, rather than slave-dependent crops such as cotton. Charles Town did, however, have frequent slave auctions. The spectacles took place on the steps of the Jefferson County Courthouse in the town square and were well attended by slave traders from Virginia, which was just over the state line. The courthouse was two stories high and topped with a gable roof and clock tower. Out front, it had a portico, white pillars, and stone steps. Men and women in chains and metal collars were marched out in front and sold to the highest bidder. Smith frequently attended slave auctions, rubbing shoulders with flesh traders in hats and long coats smoking hand-rolled cigarettes as they bid on men, women, and children. Smith endured the slave markets to purchase people and set them free. "My husband frequently demonstrated his feeling for the colored race by purchasing slaves and giving them their liberty," Pleasant recalled.

Pleasant's marriage to Smith was short-lived. Smith took ill less than two years after they were married in

*John J. J. Pleasant's original surname may have been spelled Pleasants or Pleasance. He is listed as John Pleasant in the 1850, 1860, and 1870 census, with no "s." In her dictated memoirs, Mary Ellen Pleasant refers to him as John J. Pleasant, again with no "s." However, in 1870 he registered to vote in California as John James Pleasants. While this may have been a clerical error, it could also indicate that he used both the Pleasant and Pleasants spellings of his surname.

1844. On his deathbed, he summoned his bride to his side. "Promise me," he said to his wife. "Promise me you will devote a portion of the money I leave you to the cause of freeing the slaves," he begged. "I promise with a full heart," she told him. Smith died shortly after, leaving his entire estate to Pleasant.

Smith's death left Pleasant in a familiar place; she was on her own again. In her grief, she grew closer to her late husband's land manager, John James Pleasants, or, as she called him, JJ, and the Husseys back in Nantucket. Pleasant returned to Nantucket after her husband's funeral. There, Captain Edward Gardner, a friend of the Husseys who had known her as a girl in Nantucket, helped her manage her husband's estate, selling off his various properties and assets and dealing with paperwork.

In 1846, as Pleasant was still mourning James, the island of Nantucket was struck by tragedy. The Great Fire of 1846, as it would later be called, almost burned down the entire town. The blaze started in a hat shop near Grandma Hussey's shop and spread to the docks, where barrels of whale oil were stored. The oil fed the blaze as it spread over the homes and businesses on the island. The fire melted the barrels of oil on the docks, spilling their flaming contents out into the ocean. The ocean seemed to turn to fire and made the night sky glow. When the blaze was extinguished seven hours later, it was nearly dawn. As the sun rose, people walked the streets in disbelief. More than one-third of the town's homes and businesses had been burned down, leaving more than eight hundred people homeless and even more without a way to make a living. The Nantucket Atheneum, where Frederick Douglass had spoken and risen to fame a few years earlier, was burned and nearly destroyed in the disaster.

After the fire, Nantucket declined as the center of the whaling industry, and jobs, citizens, and capital fled Massachusetts, leaving those who remained to figure out how to rebuild. Shortly after the fire, Captain Edward Gardner finished settling Pleasant's estate and gave her the proceeds, which amounted to $45,000 ($1.2 million). In 1848, Pleasant married JJ in a small ceremony in West Virginia.

Late in 1848, gold was discovered in California. Men from all over the country and the world left wives, jobs, and families behind to try to become rich in the California gold rush. President James K. Polk evangelized for men to set out for San Francisco in his State of the Union address in December 1848, which was reprinted in Nantucket and Boston papers. "The accounts of the abundance of gold in that territory [California] are of such an extraordinary character as would scarcely command belief were they not corroborated by the authentic reports of officers in the public service who have visited the mineral district and derived the facts which they detail from personal observation," he said in his national address. He added that "Labor commands a most exorbitant price and all other pursuits, but that of searching for the precious metals are abandoned. Nearly the whole of the male population of the country have gone to the gold districts."[*]

After Polk's address men began to leave Nantucket for California; whaling schooners were converted into transport ships to take them there. By 1849, more than five hundred men from Nantucket had left the island for California. Among them were Pleasant's new husband, JJ, and several members of the Hussey clan.

Deserted on Nantucket by JJ and much of her surrogate family, Pleasant made up her mind that she would go to California, too. She had connections there and now possessed a small fortune as a result of her inheritance from her first husband. She had a chance at thriving there just as the male "'49ers" were doing. Besides, she felt she needed to keep an eye on JJ.

[*] James K. Polk, Fourth Annual Message, December 5, 1848, www.presidency.ucsb.edu/ws/index.php?pid=29489.

2

King Cotton's Bastard

Inside a church made of laid stone and canopied by trees on a clearing in the woodlands of Arkansas, an enslaved woman named Emmeline was summoned to the front of the congregation to undergo a confirmation ceremony. She was purportedly the first enslaved person to undergo the ritual in the state. The faces of the congregants at the Episcopal Church of Arkansas were of slave-owning families from the cotton plantations of the western part of the state. They watched with absorption as she marched to the front of the congregation. Not only would Emmeline confirm her faith, but she would also join slave-owning men and women as a member of the congregation and a sister in Christ.

Emmeline was a fair-skinned black woman described as "the most beautiful type of creole." She
was unmarried and had two children by two different
men. That couldn't be held against her, as her body
had been sold and rented out at various points by the
family who owned her, who claimed that "she lived the
most Christian life of anyone we ever met." The confirmation ceremony consisted of a series of questions
about accepting Christ and renouncing evil, which
had to be answered affirmatively; it ended with prayers
and the laying on of hands. Emmeline's ceremony was
presided over by Bishop George Washington Freeman,
a stoic man who dressed in gray vests and jackets with
a preacher's collar on his shirt. He put his hands on
Emmeline's head and shoulders and prayed over her
as amens arose from the congregation. With this sacra-
ment, she hoped, a place would be prepared for her in
Heaven. She was near the end of her life, and she was
getting her affairs into order.

Emmeline was on borrowed time; at nearly forty
years of age, she had surpassed the normal life ex-
pectancy for an enslaved person and had lived a long
life for her era. In the 1850s, the average life span of
enslaved African Americans was between twenty-two
and thirty-six years. Between tetanus contracted from
rusted farm equipment, food- and waterborne illnesses,
sexually transmitted infections, disease-carrying mosquitoes, and hemorrhaging childbirths, enslaved people
were considered lucky to reach their thirtieth year.
Emmeline had survived dozens of outbreaks of cholera,

malaria, and yellow fever in the mosquito-infested backwater of the Mississippi delta. She had survived the doctorless births of two sons, but now she was waning, and as the year 1851 dawned on the plantation where she lived near the Arkansas-Tennessee state line, she could sense that she had entered the final stretch of her life. She had lived in one form or another of bondage since birth, and she hoped that before she joined her Lord of lords and her ancestors in the afterlife, she could secure the freedom of her children, Robert Reed Church and James Wilson.

Emmeline was born on a tobacco plantation outside Norfolk, Virginia. Her exact birth date was never recorded, but she was told she had been born about the year 1815. Her mother was an enslaved woman named Lucy. When Lucy was first sold as a girl on a slave auction block in Virginia, the slave seller claimed she was a tribal princess who had been taken from the island of Hispaniola. The rumor of royal blood would become family lore. Whether or not it was true, Lucy and her descendants would always believe they were from royalty despite their station as chattel.

For the first years of her life, Emmeline lived with her mother on a plantation in Lynchburg, Virginia, owned by a doctor named Phillip Burton. When she was a small girl, Dr. Burton gave her as a gift to his youngest daughter, Rosalie Virginia Burton. A few years later, the Burton family sold off her mother, Lucy, to a planter in Natchez, Mississippi, along with ninety-nine other slaves for more than $85,000 ($1.7 million). Emmeline's mother was sold away so early in life that Emmeline couldn't remember much about her. Rosalie, her owner, was the closest thing she had to family for most of her life. Emmeline and Rosalie were "more the order of sisters than mistress and maid," the family that owned her claimed.

When Emmeline reached womanhood, Rosalie transferred the rights to her to a white businessman from Memphis who had taken an interest in her. Captain Charles B. Church was a married man and spent most of his time away on the Mississippi River, where he commanded a fleet of steamships. Emmeline would serve as his concubine while continuing to reside with Rosalie. Captain Church would send for Emmeline when he wanted her. In 1839, their trysts produced a son.

Robert Reed Church, whom everyone called Bob, was born on June 18, 1839, on a cotton plantation outside Memphis, Tennessee. Captain Church fathered several white children with his wife, Mary Church, but Bob was his healthiest offspring. His only white children to live past infancy were Molly Church, a deaf-mute, and Charles Church Jr., who was sickly. A few years after Bob was born, Emmeline conceived another son, a boy, whom she named James Wilson. James was not Captain Church's son, however, which was obvious from his blond hair and fair skin. Captain Church was a dark-featured, dark-haired white man.

In her final days, Emmeline underwent confirmation and brokered deals for her sons to be set free after she died. James, the younger of her boys, had blue eyes.

He could pass for a white boy without much difficulty. He was described as being "as perfect a specimen of the Caucasian as could be found anywhere in the world." Emmeline planned for James to live with Rosalie after she died; Rosalie promised to pass him off as one of her own kin. Robert, on the other hand, had fair skin, narrow dark eyes, and wavy dark hair, and though he had "very little African blood," he could not have passed for white as easily as his younger brother. Emmeline had to work out a different arrangement for him.

One day, as her health was declining, Captain Church called on Emmeline. When they were in her quarters, she pleaded with him to free their son, Robert, upon her death and send him to a school for colored children in Cincinnati. Captain Church agreed, setting her mind at ease. In 1851, Emmeline finally passed away on Rosalie's plantation; in her last moments she hoped that her soul was bound for heaven and her sons would grow up free. Her death left her sons without a mother and crushed Rosalie. "I could never see as much sunshine in the after," she said.

Not long after Emmeline was buried, a horse-drawn carriage arrived on Rosalie's estate. The buggy carried Captain Charles Church, a thirty-nine-year-old white man of large stature. Church had tanned skin and dark hair that he wore parted at the side and tucked behind his ears. His face was round and boyish with small blue eyes and a downturned mouth. He wore expensive suits with ties knotted into a stubby bow around his collar. As a boy growing up in Ohio, he had become fascinated with the work of Robert Fulton, the developer of the commercially successful steamboat, and taken to the river. He skipped his later years of schooling to work in the machine rooms of steamboats and taught himself engineering and sailing. In a few years, he worked his way up to the rank of captain. Now he was successful and wealthy and owned a steamboat line, multiple properties, and several slaves. His purpose in going to Rosalie's estate was clear: he had come to the estate to take Robert away.

Robert was twelve years old when Captain Church came for him. He packed his things, said good-bye to his younger brother, James, and boarded his father's carriage. They departed down a dirt road, rolling through acres of cotton fields, leaving the life he knew behind. Reflecting on Robert's departure, Rosalie later lamented, "my love for your mother endeared her little ones to me. . . . I never intended to hold them in bondage . . . but your father promised your mother . . . he would put you in school and educate you."

Captain Church had no intention of putting Bob in school; he told him he was taking him to Memphis to put him to work aboard his steamship. There were several factors that could have influenced his rationale in breaking his promise to Robert's mother. First, he was a slaveholder; he owned at least half a dozen slaves, several of whom he used as workers on his boat. He lived in Memphis, a town of cotton warehouses, storefronts, and mansions built around four town squares named Market, Court, Auction, and Exchange, where slave traders held regular auctions. A boy Robert's age went for as much as $650 ($19,000) at the slave auction in Court Park near Captain Church's residence. Perhaps he decided his black son would be safest where he could keep an eye on him. The fugitive slave law of 1852 empowered slave traders to capture free African Americans and enslave them with or often without proof that they had ever been enslaved. It is also possible that he may have wanted Robert to be with him, his desire to leave a legacy. He had given his white son, Charles Jr., his name, but he knew it was unlikely that the sickly boy would ever follow in his footsteps on the river. Some part of him may have hoped that the strong black son, whom he had given the first name of his hero, Robert Fulton, and his own last name would follow in his footsteps, even if he knew it was unlikely that a black boy could ever be a captain or that the two of them could ever live openly as father and son. Whatever his reasons were for putting him to work, Robert had no choice in the matter.

Robert was excited when he learned he was going to Memphis. Captain Church had taken him there once years before. Robert recalled how thrilled he had been to see the hustle and bustle of the big city and looked forward to seeing it again. Robert's mother had been a house slave all her life, serving as an assistant and seamstress to Rosalie and a concubine to Captain Church. In the world Robert knew, black people could not rise past servitude. A life working on steamships was certainly at least as good as if not better than anything that awaited him on the plantation he'd left. When Robert and Captain Church got close to the riverbank in Arkansas, they could see Memphis, across the Mississippi River. They caught a ferry across the river and arrived at the Memphis wharf, a clearing on a part of the shore that curved in and created a natural harbor. There, ships arrived and departed carrying passengers and cargo. The wharf was alive with activity as dockworkers and sailors scuttled among dozens of steamships tied to the pier at the river's edge. Jugglers and newspaper boys caught the attention of travelers coming and going from the pier. This was Robert's new home.

Captain Church operated a line of steamships at the Memphis wharf, and Robert was to work and live on his vessels. He was given a job as cabin boy on Captain Church's ships. Every day, he helped the cook in the kitchen and took the officers on the ship their meals. He was also a messenger for the crew, sprinting from one end of the ship to the other to relay instructions, messages, and even jokes between the men.

Captain Church's ships were described by one customer as floating palaces. The ships chugged up and down the Mississippi, churning the river as their paddle wheels spun and splashed, powered by a steam engine housed in a boiler in the center of the ship with a chimney extending from it. Travelers spent their time in expensive salons with cut-glass chandeliers and draperies made of scarlet velvet and thickly woven silk. The window frames and doors were finished with gold-painted woodwork. The rooms were filled with easy chairs and sofas, and there was a band playing at either end of the boat.

The passengers on Captain's Church steamboats were cotton planters, wealthy families on holiday as well as gamblers. Most of them were intrigued by the presence of a child on the boat. Often they engaged Robert in conversation to pass the time or asked him to run errands in exchange for hefty tips.

In the dining room, Robert scurried about, following orders from the waiters and kitchen staff as they served fine cuts of meat with fresh vegetables, fruit, and cakes on china with sterling silver cutlery. The glasses of the travelers were kept full of sherry wine and mint julep. Passengers looked on jealously at those who were chosen to eat with Captain Church at the captain's table, where he would regale his dinner guests with stories of the river and his travels.

The captain seemed to be in multiple places at once, moving between the pilot house and the parlor. Robert caught glimpses of him charming his passengers with his sparkling blue eyes. He seemed to know each passenger by name, greeting each like an old friend.

Though Captain Church enjoyed transporting travelers up and down the river, his main source of income was transporting cotton. He transported thousands of bales of cotton at a time, stacked like bricks on the deck of the ship. Sometimes the deck was packed so full, passeners could barely find a spot to stand on if they tried to venture out of the interior of the ship onto the deck.

Cotton shippers like Captain Church were part of the global supply chain for cotton fiber. Cotton was planted, harvested, ginned, and baled into parcels by enslaved African Americans on plantations in the Mississippi delta. From there thousands of bales of cotton were loaded onto carts pulled by horses and donkeys and taken to a port along the Mississippi, where it was then loaded onto steamboats and transported to warehouses in Mississippi river towns or to St. Louis or the port of New Orleans. From the port of New Orleans or St. Louis, it was then shipped via the Atlantic Ocean to factories in New York, Massachusetts, and Manchester, England, where it was spun and woven into textiles. Cotton fiber, an industry worth $100 million a year ($20 billion), was the United States' top export and made up 60 percent of the gross domestic product. The United States' second-largest (and England's biggest) industry, textile production, depended on cotton, which was much cheaper than wool or silk. Wall Street fed tens of millions of dollars of financing into cotton growing. Planters often put up the people they enslaved as collateral to secure loans. By 1851, cotton had become so profitable that Natchez, Mississippi, the cotton-growing capital of the world, was home to half of the millionaires in the United States and per capita had the most millionaires of any town in the world, beating out New York City, Paris, and London. Robert's grandmother had been enslaved to a planter in Natchez.

Robert got along well with the adults who worked for his father aboard the ship, who seemed to take pity on him. The chambermaids mothered him and he roughhoused and played pranks with the men on the ship. "I remember your childhood capers," Kinder Blair, an Irishman whom his father employed as pastry chef, recalled. "All of us men used to play tricks on each other . . . we worked hard but we enjoyed ourselves."

Captain Church understood that Robert was a boy among men on the ship and kept an eye on him and offered him guidance. "Don't let anyone call you a nigger," he told him. "Fight if necessary to protect yourself against such insults." He taught Bob how to defend himself, telling him, "If someone strikes you, hit him back and I'll back you." "He urged me never to be a coward," Robert remembered of his father's advice on the river.

Although Captain Church never allowed Robert to refer to him as his father, he did show him affection. Once he took his son to a photographer's studio so they could get their picture taken together. For the occasion, the captain purchased matching outfits. The outfits were Knights Templar costumes, consisting of dark-colored pants and jackets with a matching hat and a sash. The hat had frills above the brim. In the matching costumes, Robert and his father looked almost identical.

After a few months on the river, the excitement of it all began to fade, and Robert felt alone. He was the only boy on the boat and never saw any other children. His mother was gone and he missed his younger brother, James, but none of that could be helped; the Mississippi was his home now.

ON MARCH 22, 1855, CAPTAIN CHURCH'S STEAMSHIP, *BULLETIN NO. 2*, was docked in Memphis, readying a large shipment of cotton. As the crew prepared the vessel to sail down the Mississippi, slaves in linen shirts and straw hats rolled bales of the cotton up a gangplank onto the boat and stacked them in six-foot-high piles on the deck.

Robert was sixteen years old and worked as a dishwasher on *Bulletin No. 2*. He had grown tall and had slick black hair, a straight nose, and a cleft chin. His eyes were small, dark, and piercing. He had taught himself to read by collecting the discarded newspapers passengers left behind. He had not learned how to write, but he could sign his name—Robert R. Church—with looping strokes. The newspapers the customers left scattered about the cabin that day carried news of the construction of a locomotive line in Memphis that would carry passengers to the gold rush in California when it was finished.

That evening, *Bulletin No. 2* was destined for Vicksburg, Mississippi, a cotton depot between Memphis and New Orleans. Men in top hats and suits and women in colorful dresses and skirts boarded *Bulletin No. 2*, alongside its crew, making their way around the piles of cotton on the deck and into the cabin house. In the kitchen Bob prepared for the dinner service that evening. Just before sunset, *Bulletin No. 2* set sail for the three-day voyage with fifty passengers, more than sixty crew, and over 3,500 bales of cotton valued at more than $100,000 ($2.6 million).

On the second day of the journey, as the ship neared Transylvania, Louisiana, Robert was in the kitchen, preparing to play a practical joke. He hid in the kitchen as a crew member came ambling in with a tall stack of dirty plates. He then jumped out and threw a handful of paprika onto the stove in front of the man, hoping to make the open flame flare up and startle him. He scurried out of the kitchen and shut the door behind him. As he listened by the door, he heard someone in the front of the ship yell, "Fire!"

While Robert was playing his prank in the kitchen, a few passengers had made their way out to the deck to smoke and get some fresh air. As they chatted and puffed cigars, an ember carried by the wind landed on one of the many bales of cotton stacked near them. When Robert ran to the deck he saw several bales of cotton on fire. The crew grabbed buckets and threw water on the cotton, but the blaze spread faster than they could haul water, and before long the whole boat seemed to be on fire. Captain Church had neglected to equip the ship with a working water pump and fire hose, and fighting the fire without them was a losing effort. Captain Church appeared on the deck. "Run the boat aground!" he commanded the ship's pilot. The ship steered toward the riverbank.

When the boat arrived at the shore, the crew fastened it to the bank with a rope. Robert then went to the aid of the women, helping them off the ship and onto the shore. Once all the female passengers were on land, he ran around to the other side of the boat, where he ran into the captain, who was supervising as his men pushed the flaming cotton bales off the boat and into the river. Captain Church noticed one passenger still on board. The man was standing in the cabin calmly looking out at the flames around him. "Save yourself!" the captain told him. "Make yourself easy, Captain," the passenger replied as the flames smoldered around him. Out of the corner of his eye, Bob noticed that one of the flaming bales that had been pushed overboard was floating back around on the river toward the shore, near the rope that was anchoring the boat. Before he could react, the bale brushed the rope and set it aflame. The burning twine eventually snapped, and one of the crew members grabbed it, straining to hold the ship to the shore with brute strength. Bob jumped off the boat and swam to the bank. The man finally lost his grip on the rope, and the boat began drifting from the bank with most of the crew still aboard.

As the boat floated farther and farther from shore, Captain Church yelled for everyone aboard to jump ship and grab a floating bale of cotton. They jumped into the river and grabbed bales, which they used as floats. A few of the chambermaids used their hoopskirts to float on the river. The skirts were held into a fashionable shape with a scaffolding that projected the fabric away from their legs, and in the water the opened-out skirts acted as flotation devices. In a matter of minutes, the boat was engulfed in flames and had drifted more than two hundred feet from the bank into the river. The man who had been standing in the cabin among the flames at last came out to the deck. He turned to Captain Church, said, "Now, gallows, save your own!" and leaped from the boat into the water.

Captain Church remained on the boat with four of his other slaves and worked to help those remaining on board. The boat continued to drift into the river until he gave up and jumped. He left four of his slaves behind in the flames. They, along with twenty-one other people, died in the fire that night. Bob watched from the bank as *Bulletin No. 2* burned and then finally sank into the Mississippi. He hoped, perhaps for the first time, to escape life as his father's slave on the river.

3

Funding the Insurrection

Fog blanketed the bay as a steamship carrying Mary Ellen Pleasant coasted toward the San Francisco pier one spring afternoon. The harbor was crowded with hundreds of ships, forming a forest of masts and sailcloth, as well as dozens of abandoned vessels, rotting and sinking into the water. Late in the afternoon on April 7, 1852, the SS *Oregon* navigated the harbor traffic and docked after a two-month trip from the East.

When Pleasant planted her feet on California soil, rats scurried near her path on the landing, which was littered with trash and horse manure. The air was cool, and it had just begun to rain. The afternoon showers liquefied the pier's landing and the streets, which were made of dirt and sand, turning them into mud.

Pleasant hailed a porter and a carriage to go into the city. As she recovered her land legs, she noticed the eyes of the people at the harbor peering in her direction. As she stared back, it began to settle on her that she was in a land that was simultaneously familiar and alien.

The faces of the crowd in San Francisco were overwhelmingly those of white men. They were a familiar class—Pleasant had grown up catering to their type as a young shop clerk in Nantucket—but as she moved through the harbor into the city, it became clear that the white men who filled the streets of San Francisco were different from the reserved Quakers of Nantucket. The city stretched out for three miles from a cluster of warehouses and fisheries at the pier on dirt roads that crisscrossed and ran up the town's hills into a metropolis of fire-brick buildings and wood-frame houses that held rooming houses, saloons, banks, and shops. The gents at the pier and in the streets spoke loudly and profanely, with accents from the far corners of the world: New England, the South, Australia, and Central America. They had been lured to California by the promise of wealth in the gold rush. It was the same siren song that had called JJ away.

The men she saw in the streets were both rugged and ornate. They draped themselves in broadcloth suits with bowler hats, underneath which they wore shirts stained with dirt and tobacco spittle. The spoils of the gold rush were evident on their bodies: gold pocket watch chains, diamond-encrusted buttons on their shirts, and gold teeth dotting their smiles. Many of the men wandered the streets intoxicated, bellowing and catcalling as they bounced among gambling houses, saloons, and theaters until they finally retired to cramped, flea-infested boardinghouses, where they slept on hard cots in common rooms.

There was a handful of women in the streets near the harbor and clustered in the saloons in town. They were white, Hispanic, and Chinese, and they were dressed elegantly, with their necks and collarbones exposed in off-shoulder dresses and their hair pinned up. Pleasant would come to know these women as "entertainers," managed by men called Macks who always lingered nigh. A woman walking down the street by herself was often such an event that men would call out, "Woman on the sidewalk!" emptying out buildings, drawing men to come and gawk at her.

Pleasant stayed in a boardinghouse operated by a friend from Massachusetts on Washington Street in an area called Sydney Town. The area was near the pier and was made up of boardinghouses constructed from converted warehouses and abandoned ships dragged from the pier. The alleys were patrolled by thieves and muggers. Sydney Town was the stomping ground for the Sydney Ducks, a gang made up of immigrants from the British penal colony in Australia. The area was also home to black and Irish workers, who, due to the surging housing prices during the gold rush, couldn't afford to live anywhere else. Pleasant found lodging in the company of friends, which she hoped would help her avoid trouble in her new home.

In her first days after she settled in the city, she got

a fix on her husband, JJ: he had gotten a job as a cook on a steamship that operated between California and Panama. Pleasant decided to try to find her own fortune in California. As a black woman in the gold rush, and one of means, she intuited that her best opportunity to make money would be as an investor.

So she became a moneylender. San Franciscans seemed always to need capital. Some were just getting started in the city after having spent their life savings to get to California; others were spendthrifts, blowing through their money almost as soon as they earned it, bingeing on prostitutes, gambling, and liquor. The cash-strapped nature of her fellow Californians provided an opportunity to Pleasant, who came to the city with plenty of money. She gave some of it to connected men and let them lend it out at 10 percent interest per month. Ten percent a month was a rate that, when collected upon, would more than double her capital every year.

Pleasant navigated the town's streets on foot or by carriage, carrying thousands of dollars of currency with her at a time, moving between the Victorian homes of the north to the rough streets in the city's south, making deposits and withdrawals. "I divided this money between Fred Longford, William West of West & Harper," she began. After dropping off money and picking up her interest payments, she then continued to "Thomas Randolph who lived on Green Street, between Stockton and Dupont." Randolph operated in North Beach, a wealthy enclave on the city's northern shore known for its hills and a Russian cemetery, where the area's children played among the grave markers. "I had known these gentlemen from home. We put our money out at ten percent interest per month," she reminisced. "Those were the good times of '49."

In addition to lending money, Pleasant peddled silver. She had connections with silver buyers and sold large quantities at good margins. "I always had friends in places where a good deal of silver was required," she recalled. One of her greatest strengths was making friends, from her days as a shop clerk in Nantucket when she had "let books alone" and "decided to study men and women." She became a master of human connection. Her ability to bond with others took her from shop clerk to wife of a wealthy man. As a widow she found another man, Captain Edward Gardner, to liquidate her late husband's estate. Pleasant had made friends everywhere she went, from Nantucket to Boston, and now she did the same in the international town of San Francisco. "When I have attached myself to one as a friend, I have remained to the end," she later said. Her networking ability allowed her to set up businesses lending out money and selling silver, which above all else required knowing the right people who knew the right people.

One of the ways she got her hands on silver was to sell and ship gold to Panama, receiving silver in return. "I did an exchange business with Panama sending down $1000 of gold [$26,000] at different times and having it changed into silver," she recalled. "Gold was then at a high premium," she continued, and in San Francisco she could get her hands on large quantities of it.

Pleasant also got her hands on silver through California's banks. She would routinely make her way to San Francisco's financial district, a series of banks and shops near the pier, where she would enter the Wells Fargo & Co. bank. The bank was a rectangular fire-brick building with wood-shuttered windows. Men in top hats and jackets and the company's stagecoach were frequently out front. Inside there was a large storeroom in the front, paneled with dark wood, and a counter in the back with a large scale on it. "My custom was to deposit gold and draw out silver, by which means I was able to turn my money over rapidly," Pleasant remembered. Once Pleasant had acquired as much silver as she could get her hands on in San Francisco she found buyers to purchase the silver for an incrementally higher price than she paid for it. The difference in price accumulated over multiple transactions into tens of thousands of dollars of profit. In her early days in San Francisco Pleasant was making between $15,000 and $25,000 a year ($392,000 and $650,000, respectively). By 1858, she was worth more than $150,000 ($4.2 million).

Her success as an investor was a mystery. Some speculated that she had such good fortune through voodoo. Others speculated that she learned to invest by trading sex for financial advice with San Francisco's rich bachelors. Another popular rumor said she eavesdropped on business conversations during the dinners she catered. "I have never been given to explaining away lies, and you can't explain away the truth," she would say. The truth is that the gold rush was an opportunity that the circumstances of Pleasant's life up until that point had prepared her for. Having been reared in a boomtown that featured women and African Americans taking part in its prosperity, Pleasant had used her days in the whaling years of Nantucket to prepare her for gold rush San Francisco. In many ways, her success was not unusual; many of the most successful participants in the gold rush came from whaling towns such as Nantucket and New Bedford. Nonetheless, for decades going forward, the brilliant black gold rush investor would confound racial stereotypes and popular explanation.

MARY ELLEN PLEASANT'S MOVES WHEN SHE ARRIVED IN SAN FRANcisco were shrewd but unspectacular. Those whom she made her money off likely did not even know she existed. As a woman and an African American, she had been discriminated against and overlooked most of her life. By the time she arrived in San Francisco, she had learned to work in the background. Moving out west allowed her to keep an eye on her new husband, grow her bequest, and make plans without drawing any more attention to herself than necessary. But what was she planning on for the long run?

Life in California was profitable, but she missed her home and the struggle back east. There had to be a purpose to it all, besides keeping tabs on JJ. Pleasant was disconnected from her old life, but she willed what pieces of home she could to her surroundings. She socialized with other Nantucketers and Bostonians. She made her favorite dishes, serving pineapple upside-down cake and honey-baked ham for friends at the private dinners and banquets she catered for extra income. She corresponded long distance with friends. She also made special efforts to procure abolitionist periodicals such as William Lloyd Garrison's *The Liberator* and *Frederick Douglass' Paper* from the East.

In the spring of 1852, as her wealth increased, *Frederick Douglass' Paper* printed a series of essays on black wealth. The series, by James McCune Smith, a public intellectual and the first African American to earn a medical degree, pondered whether free blacks should use their liberty to pursue wealth, abolition, and civil rights. "Hundred thousand dollar black men would be no better than hundred thousand dollar white men," he wrote. "Gold freezes up the humanities and all their surroundings. The wealthy are never a progressive class; they are by necessity conservatives."

In one installment Smith compared Samuel Ringgold Ward, an abolitionist, and Jeremiah Hamilton, the richest black man in New York, asking who was the better man. Ward was an abolitionist whom Pleasant knew through his nephew Rev. Thomas Marcus Decatur Ward; he lived in San Francisco and presided over the African Methodist Episcopal Church where Pleasant worshipped. Hamilton was a free black man, and like Pleasant, he was an investor. He was worth at least half a million dollars and lived in a brownstone in lower Manhattan. Hamilton shunned abolitionist causes and, like Pleasant's first husband, defined his race as Cuban.

> *Compare Sam Ward with the only black millionaire*
> *in New York, I mean Jerry Hamilton; and it is plain*
> *that manhood is a "nobler ideal" than money. The*
> *former has illustrated his people and his country, the*
> *other has fled from his identity (to use the elegant*
> *phraseology of Ethiop), like a dog with a tin kettle tied*
> *to his tail!*

Wealth and activism were binary characteristics, Smith argued in the United States' most distributed black newspaper of the antebellum period. One could either seek liberation or seek wealth, not both. As she often did when presented with two conflicting ideas, Pleasant harmonized them as only she could. She set her mind to pursue wealth but to the end of using the money she made to seek liberation for slaves, as she had promised her husband to do. Around the time that Smith printed his treatise on Hamilton and Ward, Pleasant began to become interested in a name she saw printed in the papers: John Brown.

John Brown was the most belligerent opponent of slavery since Nat Turner earlier in the century. He was a white shepherd and Calvinist preacher who believed that God wanted him to bring an end to slavery. He first made headlines when he founded an armed security force in Springfield, Massachusetts, called the League of Gileadites, the local branch of a national organization, to defend runaway slaves. William Wells Brown, an acquaintance of Pleasant, wrote on encountering the League of Gileadites on a visit to Springfield, "[W]e found there some ten or fifteen blacks, all armed to the teeth and swearing vengeance upon the heads of any who should attempt to take them."

In 1854, President Franklin Pierce, an anti-abolitionist Democrat, signed the Kansas-Nebraska Act into law, sending slavery's opponents into a fury. The law, authored by Illinois senator Stephen A. Douglas, created the territories of Kansas and Nebraska but also allowed for the expansion of slavery into the North, where it had been banned since 1819. Slavery would be permitted or banned in Kansas, a northern territory, based on a popular vote among white males in the territory. The law would potentially reintroduce slavery into the North, endangering freedmen and -women and reinforcing slavery's grip on America. Frederick Douglass and William Lloyd Garrison published angry treatises against it in their papers. On the steps of the courthouse in Peoria, Illinois, a largely unknown politician named Abraham Lincoln gave a three-hour speech decrying the law. "I hate it because of the monstrous injustice of slavery itself. I hate it because it deprives our republican example of its just influence in the world," he told hundreds of onlookers. Afterward, his Peoria speech became a thing of legend that catapulted him into national prominence.

Pleasant kept abreast of the developments. Proslavery and antislavery supporters rushed into the territory to try to influence the outcome, and the tug-of-war eventually became violent. Brown's name reappeared in the papers when he and his sons went to Kansas to lead the fight during "Bleeding Kansas," a battle between slave owners and abolitionists. After rumors circulated that he had been killed during Bleeding Kansas, he surfaced with an essay entitled "Parallels" that was published in several abolitionist papers:

> *On Sunday, the 19th of December, a negro called Jim came over to the Osage settlement from Missouri and stated that he together with his wife, two children, and another negro man were to be sold within a day or two and begged for help to get away. On Monday (the following) night, two small companies were made up to go to Missouri and forcibly liberate the five slaves together with other slaves. One of these companies I assumed to direct. We proceeded to the place, surrounded the buildings, liberated the slaves, and also took certain property supposed to belong to the estate.*
>
> *We, however, learned before leaving that a portion of the articles we had taken belonged to a man living on the plantation as a tenant, and who was supposed to have no interest in the estate. We promptly returned to him all we had taken. We then went to*

*another plantation where we freed five more slaves,
took some property and two white men. We moved very
slowly away into the Territory for some distance and
then sent the white men back, telling them to follow
as soon as they chose to do so. The other company
freed one female slave, took some property, and as I
am informed, killed one white man (the master), who
fought against the liberation.*

*Now for a comparison. Eleven persons were
forcibly restored to their natural and inalienable
rights, with but one man killed, and all "Hell is
stirred from beneath." It is currently reported that the
Governor of Missouri has made a requisition upon
the Governor of Kansas for the delivery of such as
were concerned in the last-named "dreadful outrage."
The marshal of Kansas is said to be collecting a
posse of Missouri (not Kansas) men at West Point
in Missouri, a little town about ten miles distant,
to "enforce the laws." All proslavery, conservative
free-state, and dough-faced men, and administration
tools, are filled with holy horror.*

Brown took the slave he freed to Ontario and then
disappeared into hiding. Shortly after Brown published
"Parallels," Pleasant considered leaving San Francisco for
the free black settlements in Ontario. There she hoped
she could learn how to find him. "I had no well-defined
idea of just how I was to help John and concluded to
see what could be done after I reached [Canada]," she
recalled.

AS PLEASANT WAS MAKING PLANS TO HELP BROWN STRIKE A BLOW against slavery, the rights of minorities in California were eroding. The pull of California's prosperity made it diverse, drawing people from all races, regions, and backgrounds to San Francisco. Many white men, however, saw the Hispanics, blacks, and Chinese immigrants who were present in large numbers in the city as stealers of white men's jobs and opportunities. Minorities were blamed for the city's crime and forced to live in ghettos, while taxes and legal restrictions on immigrants were made into law. In a landmark case in 1854, the California Supreme Court passed a law that banned blacks, Indians, and Chinese from testifying against white men in court. The ruling coincided with a high-profile lawsuit, *Folsom v. Leidesdorff*, in which the family of the deceased black millionaire industrialist William Leidesdorff was suing the prominent white Californian Joseph Folsom. Leidesdorff's family claimed that Folsom had conned them into signing over the Leidesdorff estate to him. Leidesdorff's black family members' testimony in the suit was deemed inadmissible, making mounting a case difficult. Pleasant donated to the effort to overturn the laws that disenfranchised minorities but kept her focus on a bigger fight: the struggle to end slavery.

LATE IN MARCH 1858, THERE WAS A KNOCK AT PLEASANT'S DOOR AT her and her husband's dwelling in San Francisco. On the other side was a portly young man named William Alvord. He gave her two steamship tickets for New York. She had learned that John Brown was going to address an African American expatriate community in Chatham, Ontario, in Canada and had decided to go there and try to meet him. She sent out a few letters and withdrew a large sum of money before she left. "I took with me in addition to the money needed for expenses, a thirty-thousand-dollar US Treasury draft, which I decided to give to John Brown," she recalled.

On April 5, 1858, Pleasant and JJ went to the San Francisco pier and boarded a steamship for New York. The ship dropped anchor in the East River and docked at a crowded port on the east side of Manhattan. Pleasant's old friend Captain Edward Gardner received the couple. Gardner had dark hair and a clean-shaven face and was dressed in a dark suit. He looked much older than when Pleasant had last seen him; the skin of his face drooped around his eyes, chin, and cheeks.

Gardner took Pleasant and JJ into town and helped get them set up at a colored boardinghouse. Pleasant did not want to spend too much time in New York before beginning the final leg of their trip. Her plan was to take the money she had brought for John Brown and convert it into a draft on a Canadian bank. After she did so, she and JJ caught a steamboat at New York Harbor that night for Chatham, a town just across the Detroit

River on the Canadian side of the border, where she hoped to find John Brown.

CHATHAM WAS A TOWN OF FARMS AND SMALL SHOPS BUILT ALONG the Thames River, and the train tracks ran along it. When Pleasant arrived, the city already had a large population of blacks composed of runaway slaves and expatriate freedmen from America. In May 1858, John Brown came to town to meet with the black population for what he called a Provisional Constitutional Convention. More than forty Chatham residents met in a schoolhouse in secret, away from the gaze of the white residents. They told the townspeople they were meeting to discuss the formation of a new Masonic lodge. Their plan backfired as curious townspeople gathered around the schoolhouse, peering in the windows.

They convened just after 10 a.m. Dr. Martin Delany, a black man with thinning hair, dark skin, and downturned eyes, stood to address the attendees. They were there to discuss a plan to form a new free territory in West Virginia. After Delany, Brown stood to explain his scheme in detail. As he began to speak, he was interrupted by Delany, who insisted that everyone swear an oath of secrecy before Brown revealed anything. "I solemnly affirm that I will not in any way divulge any of the secrets of this convention, except to persons entitled to know the same, on the pain of forfeiting the respect and protection of this organization," he stated. The attendees repeated the oath after him.

Brown told the gathering that he planned to form a militia in West Virginia, liberate several slave plantations, and establish a free territory and military stronghold in the Appalachian Mountains. It would be a place slaves could escape to, a permanently free, multiracial community. He assured his listeners that his plan would be successful because he had been studying insurrectionary warfare, particularly the history of the Haitian Revolution and the military strategy of Toussaint L'Ouverture. He planned to establish the territory by staging a slave insurrection in West Virginia after he sacked the US armory in Harpers Ferry for weapons. He also had a provisional constitution he had written for the new region read aloud. It was voted on and ratified. The men and women present hugged and thumped one another on the back in congratulations.

The next day the convention convened again at 6 p.m. for provisional elections for the new territory. John Brown was nominated and confirmed as commander in chief of the new region, and a freeman named J. H. Kagi was named secretary of war. The convention's attendees could not agree on who would be president and argued until nine the next morning. After a recess they reconvened, and Brown suggested that they postpone selecting a president. The motion carried. They then elected members of Congress from the attendees and adjourned at 2 p.m.

Following the meeting, Mary Ellen Pleasant arranged to have a one-on-one with John Brown. At the meeting she gave him a bank draft for $45,000 ($1.3 million). "I turned the whole amount over to John Brown and his son one night in my room," she later said. They then went over the details of Brown's plan. "John Brown and I talked it over but we did not confide the details to our friends." Pleasant knew many of slaves on the West Virginia plantations. She told Brown she would help spread the word of the planned slave revolt. "I told him that by the time he had organized for his fight I would have the blacks in a state of insurrection and near at hand to come in with reinforcements," she recalled. "With this agreement, we parted."

After the convention, Mary Ellen Pleasant and JJ began to put down roots in Canada. After meeting Brown, she traveled to Montreal for an abolitionist convention, where she met up with some of her and her husband's old friends. "Wendell Phillips and Geo Green called on me in Montreal, but I did not tell them of my plans with Brown," she recalled. "I know there was to be bloodshed and concluded not to talk it over with them." She wanted to keep Brown's insurrection and her role in it a secret.

Pleasant left Canada and traveled to West Virginia, where she went from plantation to plantation, talking with the slaves about Brown's plan for a revolt. "They were very much taken with the idea of participating in the fight for their freedom," she recalled.

The fall after the convention, she and JJ returned to Canada and purchased four connected lots of land overlooking the Thames River to build a homestead. She also purchased a silver revolver with a long barrel and joined the Chatham Vigilance Committee and Militia with the aim of protecting the black community in Chatham. There were fourteen members of the militia. Joining them were the organizers of the Brown meeting, Martin Delany, and the abolitionist publishers William Howard Day and Mary Ann Shadd Cary, all of whom had relocated to Chatham around the same time as the Pleasants.

In the fall of 1858, a slave catcher kidnapped a teenage black boy in London, Ontario, a few miles up the tracks from Chatham. The fourteen members of the vigilance committee were alerted and met at the train tracks carrying their weapons. When the train arrived, they boarded it and searched for the boy. They found him in the back of the train, seated next to his captor. At gunpoint, they removed him from the train and retreated back into Chatham.

AFTER THE TRAIN RESCUE, PLEASANT WAS INVIGORATED AND BE-gan writing to John Brown in anticipation of his revolt. "The ax is laid at the root of the tree. When the first blow is struck there will be more money and help," she wrote.

John Brown began his raid the month after the

train robbery, to the dismay of his collaborators, whom he had promised he would wait until he was better prepared. He was undersupplied and undermanned, with only eighteen men in his militia and a small supply of artillery. In the first hours, they were successful: he and his men captured hostages, including George Washington's great-grandnephew Lewis Washington, and took control of the areas surrounding the armory by early the next morning. Brown had hoped that word of his effort would spread to local slaves, who would come to his aid to reinforce their ranks. They, however, were unaware of what was happening. By the afternoon, Brown and his men were surrounded by a local militia and holed up in a barn. A day later, they were captured.

Pleasant was devastated when she learned that his plan had been foiled. "I was astounded when I heard that he had started in and was beaten and captured and that the affair upon which I had staked my money and built so much hope was a fiasco," she recalled. Her disbelief turned to worry when she realized that she was in danger if it were found out that she had helped Brown. "We began to look about for our own safety, for we read in the papers that all of Brown's fellow conspirators were being sought for by the authorities. When they captured him they found among his papers a letter from me."

A year after his failed raid, Brown was tried and executed by hanging. "I often wished that I went up on that scaffold with him," she lamented. For the time being, she went into hiding and tried to figure out what she would do next.

4

Robert Reed Church and the Civil War

As the shock of John Brown's raid and execution spread across the country, Captain Charles Church was doubling down on his cotton-shipping business. In 1858, he bought a new steamboat. It was massive at two hundred tons and had two engines. The interior was furnished with chaises, lounges, and armchairs. It had parlors, dining rooms, kitchens, and dozens of sleeping cabins. The exterior of the boat had a wide deck large enough to accommodate thousands of bales of cotton. Captain Church christened his new boat the *Victoria* and put her into service on the Mississippi River from St. Louis to New Orleans, with a stopover in Memphis.

The captain made Robert Reed Church a steward aboard the new vessel. The rank of steward was the highest possible for a slave. Robert was nineteen years old and had spent the last seven years on the river in the kitchens and dining rooms of Captain Church's boats to earn the promotion. During that time, he and the captain had grown fond of each other. "My father gave me anything I wanted," Robert remembered. "Though he doesn't openly recognize me," he equivocated. Earlier in the year, Captain Church's other son, Charles Jr., died at the age of ten, resting the legacy of the Church name on Robert, Captain Church's bastard son and slave.

In his work aboard the ships, Robert became acquainted with a porter, named Blanche K. Bruce, who worked the docks. Like Robert, Bruce was the product of a tryst between a white slave owner and his female slave. Unlike Robert, his father had freed him and sent him to school. Bruce was stout with light brown skin and short, wavy hair. In Bruce, Robert perhaps saw an alternative version of himself, were he free. The two became fast friends, and Robert allowed himself to dream of freedom.

As a steward, Robert was put in charge of the ship's kitchen and dining room. The role put him on an equal footing with white merchants. When the ship docked, Robert, usually accompanied by Captain Church, would meet with grocers, importers, and bakers to buy meat, vegetables, fruit, liquor, bread, and cakes. His work was held to a high standard, as the meals on Captain Church's boats were legendary. "The markets were searched for the best the country afforded and the days on board were marked by one feast after another."

Captain Church also set Robert up with a woman. The *Victoria* was often filled with young white women who were part of bridal parties. Sometimes there were as many as five groups of bachelorettes aboard at once. Though in general Captain Church may have given Robert whatever he wanted, the young women who were guests on the captain's ship were off-limits. Just after Robert turned eighteen, Captain Church arranged for Robert to have a "slave marriage" with a woman named Margaret Pico who was owned by friends of his in New Orleans. Marriages arranged between people owned by slaveholders were explicitly sexual in nature, as the expectation was that the coupling would result in children and produce more slaves for the owners.

Captain Church often lodged with the family that owned Margaret when he spent a few days in New Orleans at the end of the *Victoria*'s run. After Robert and Margaret's marriage was arranged, whenever the captain and his son went to New Orleans, the captain would deposit Robert in Margaret's slave quarters, where he would spend the duration of their stay in New Orleans. In 1859, Robert and Margaret produced a daughter, whom they named Laura.

In the fall of 1860, Abraham Lincoln's victory in the presidential election sent shock waves through the South, setting off a chain of events that would lead to the Civil War. Captain Church's steamship line was entangled with slavery. His business relied on shipping cotton picked on slave plantations to ports along the

Mississippi. Talk of war could be heard among the passengers as Bob walked the dining halls on board the ships during meal service.

On April 19, 1961, in the first days of the Civil War, President Lincoln ordered the Union Navy to blockade all Southern waterways, cutting off the South's trade with Europe and interfering with the Confederacy's transportation of troops and provisions on the waterways. Lincoln deployed five hundred warships to ports in the Atlantic Ocean and on the Mississippi and Ohio Rivers to destroy any Confederate ships carrying supplies.

Not long after the blockade was announced, Robert was on board the *Victoria* when a group of Confederate sailors wearing gray military uniforms boarded the ship. The men announced that they were commandeering the ship on behalf of the Confederate Navy. "My sympathies were with the Union, though I did own slaves," the captain claimed, saying he was given no choice but to turn over his ship with his black son aboard it. The Confederacy renamed his boat Confederate Steamship *Victoria.*

Robert was conscripted to the CSS *Victoria* in the employ of the rebel navy. The boat was used to transport troops and military supplies up and down the Mississippi, using its speed to outrun the blockade fleet. If a ship was caught, the Union Navy had instructions to destroy and sink it. While Bob was working on a Confederate blockade runner, his younger brother, James Wilson, was conscripted into the Confederate Army as a soldier in Arkansas. Emmeline had hoped during her dying days to save her sons from slavery, and now they found themselves aiding the Confederacy in the war to protect the right of white Southerners to hold black men like themselves in bondage.

NEAR DAYBREAK ON JUNE 6, 1862, AS THE SUN WAS RISING OVER the Mississippi River, Robert Reed Church was on the deck of the CSS *Victoria*. His ship was floating just outside the Memphis wharf, looking out onto a fleet of Confederate warships further out on the river, waiting for a coming battle. The Union Navy was approaching to invade and conquer Memphis. Robert stood on the deck with crew members and Confederate sailors, watching the approaching fleet draw closer, feeling both uncertainty and excitement. The Union warships would perhaps bring freedom if they were victorious, but they also could bring death if they sank his ship.

There were eight Confederate ships in the river guarding the city. Each of them had cotton bales stacked like bricks against all four sides of their superstructures to protect against light artillery. The cotton-clad flotilla was poorly armed. In total, the rebel ships had eight cannons. The Union fleet was twice the size of the Confederate. Its seventeen ships were assembled in two battle lines moving down the river, their exteriors clad with iron, armed with guns and cannon. In another line were nine ram boats with six-foot-long knifelike structures on their front end. Those "beaks" could puncture the hulls of the enemy ships when smashed into them, flooding and sinking them.

In the early morning, more than five thousand Memphians made their way from their homes to the edge of the river to watch the battle. They stood in groups on the bluffs, twenty feet up from the fighting. The Union fleet stopped two hundred feet from the city; then the air exploded with the steady drone of gunfire. "About 5½ A.M., the Bragg came up toward us and opened fire," a Confederate soldier later reported. "It was answered by us instantly." The fleets exchanged fire for more than an hour with neither side taking much damage. By the time they were done, the river was covered in smoke and the air smelled of gunpowder. In the haze, two Union ram boats came charging toward the Confederate ships. They knifed at their hulls, sinking one, the CSS *Colonel Lovell,* and damaged several others, puncturing their hulls. As the Confederate ships scrambled, the Union gunboats sailed into deadly range of the Confederate ships and opened fire.

The Union ships shot up and breached one Confederate ship after another. On the bluff, the citizens of Memphis, who had been cheering the gunfight, fell silent. After the Union Navy sank three Confederate ships, the Confederate flotilla surrendered. When the battle was over, a union ship began to close on Robert's ship, the CSS *Victoria.* Something inside Robert told him to flee. He followed his instinct; he walked to the edge of the boat, gathered his nerve, and jumped. With a splash, he disappeared into the Mississippi as the sun came up over Memphis.

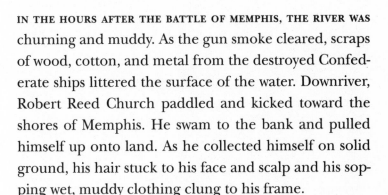

IN THE HOURS AFTER THE BATTLE OF MEMPHIS, THE RIVER WAS churning and muddy. As the gun smoke cleared, scraps of wood, cotton, and metal from the destroyed Confederate ships littered the surface of the water. Downriver, Robert Reed Church paddled and kicked toward the shores of Memphis. He swam to the bank and pulled himself up onto land. As he collected himself on solid ground, his hair stuck to his face and scalp and his sopping wet, muddy clothing clung to his frame.

What was he at that moment? A slave, a freedman, a deserter? Whom did he belong to? The Confederacy, the Union, his father, himself? There was only one way to be sure. He collected himself and headed toward the city, dripping water as if he had just been baptized. He was unafraid of whatever awaited him. He had just survived his second flirtation with a watery grave. Slavery and brushes with death had wrung whatever fear he had been born with from his breast.

In Memphis, Robert found men both black and white wearing blue Union uniforms and carrying guns, stationed on corners, patrolling the town. High in the sky, he could see the Union flag flying over city hall. After the battle of Memphis, the mayor surrendered the city to the Union, suspending slavery in the town. At that moment Robert dared to think he was free.

5

The Near Lynching of a Millionaire

July 1863

Late one hot evening in New York City, a lynch mob made up of white men and adolescent boys marched down East 29th Street in Manhattan toward the home of New York's richest black man, Jeremiah Hamilton. They wore dingy shirts with the sleeves rolled up and leather boots and carried revolvers, rifles, clubs, and sharpened sticks. As they marched down the gravel street toward the brownstone where Hamilton lived, they bellowed out his house number, "Sixty-eight! Sixty-eight! Sixty-eight!" and waved their weapons above their heads.

Hamilton and his wife, Eliza, heard the chants reverberating through the walls of their home. Hamilton was perhaps New York's most infamous African American man. He was a ruthless Wall Street broker, lived in a brownstone in an all-white section of the city, and was married to a white woman fifteen years his junior. His skin was the color of mahogany; he wore expensive gray-and-black suits and a wig of flowing black hair. He was referred to as the Prince of Darkness and Nigger Hamilton as the newspapers cataloged his financial and social dealings in New York.

He could hear the boots of the men down on the street and their yelling and taunts as they drew closer to his house. Out of options, he bolted out the back door, jumped the back fence of his house, and ran away down 28th Street. As the men drew closer, Eliza was left behind to face the mob alone.

The streets had been a war zone for two days, ever since the federal government had begun draft lotteries for the Civil War. After the first names were drawn in New York, the city exploded in violence as working-class white men took to the streets and raged against the prospect of being forced to fight and end the enslavement of African Americans. In mobs of thousands, they overpowered the police, destroyed government buildings, lynched and crucified black citizens, and destroyed black churches and orphanages. High-profile African Americans were hunted as prize kills for lynch mobs. The day before they set upon Hamilton's home, rioters had sacked and burned a pharmacy that belonged to James McCune Smith, America's first black medical doctor.

When they arrived at Hamilton's house, the men began to scream, "Bring the nigger out!" One of Hamilton's white neighbors came outside and told the mob he wasn't home, but the mob ignored his pleas to leave and continued shouting, "Nigger!" and "Bring him out!" One of the men told the neighbor, "There's a nigger living in there with two white women, and we are going to bring him out and hang him from the lamp post."

The men climbed Hamilton's stoop and began slamming their shoulders into the front door. When it wouldn't give, one of the men ran around the back of the house and rammed in the basement door. He ran up the stairs into the parlor floor of the house, followed by a dozen other rioters. At the top of the stairs, they were met by Eliza Jane Hamilton. Eliza was tall with pale skin, a downturned mouth, and brown hair that she wore in a French braid. "What do you want?" she asked the men. "Mr. Hamilton," one man grunted. "We're going to kill him," another threatened. "Why?" Eliza demanded, trying to appear unafraid. "Revenge!" another man yelled. The men pushed past Eliza and spread out across the house to look for Hamilton. They scoured the house's five bedrooms, its long hallways, its closets, the basement, the dining room, and the parlor for the rich black man they had come to lynch. Along the way, they looted his home, stuffing items of value they found in the house into their shirts and pockets.

Observing the commotion through their blinds, his neighbors locked their doors and bolted their windows. Two neighbors came outside and stood on their stoops to see what was going on.

"There's trouble at the Hamiltons', and they purport that they were going to burn him out and hang him," the first neighbor said.

"Will you go down?" the other neighbor asked.

"No."

"You won't stand here and see a man murdered without going to help him?" the neighbor asked after a break in the conversation. The other neighbor didn't answer.

Inside the house, a man with a revolver came downstairs and confronted Eliza. "Give us all your liquor and cigars," he demanded. "I have no liquor," she told them. "I have cider." She went to fetch the cigars and cider. The looting went on for half an hour, and it seemed as though the men had no intention of leaving. Some of the men sat down on Hamilton's parlor chairs, chaises, and sofas and put their feet up, smoking cigars and guzzling cider. Forty-five minutes later, the men became convinced that Hamilton wasn't there and concluded that they had stolen all that there was to steal. One by one, they finally gave up and left.

Hamilton, the richest black man in New York, narrowly escaped death that day. However, it was the fleetness of his feet and not his wealth and talent that saved his life. There had been a time when he believed that his money would protect him from racism. His brush with death at the hands of a white mob was perhaps proof that African Americans, even if they had the opportunity and skill to amass a fortune, would still face threats to their lives and prosperity, similar to the ones the masses of African Americans faced, perhaps greater because of their stature.

Hamilton died in his seventies, a decade after the Civil War ended. At the time of his death in 1875, he had a net worth of nearly a million dollars, making him, at that time, the richest black man in the United States.

Freedom and Progress

*If there be any who are afraid of the
rivalry of the black man in office or
in business, I have only to advise
them to try and beat their competitor.*
—THADDEUS STEVENS, 1867

6

Forty Acres Deferred

According to lore, on a hot day in June 1865, at the end of the Civil War, a group of Union soldiers on horseback rode into Oklahoma from Texas and convened groups of enslaved African Americans in clearings in the woods and on plantation fields. In the thick, dust-filled summer air, they told the gathering of African Americans that slavery was over. Oklahoma was vast, full of frontier towns, farms, and Indian settlements. More than five thousand African Americans lived in the territory in bondage. Despite what they may have been told, African Americans in Oklahoma would not be liberated until much later.

They had been enslaved not by white men but by the Indians of the Creek, Choctaw, Cherokee, Chickasaw, and Seminole tribes who ruled the region. The people of the five major tribes of Oklahoma fought

with the Confederacy during the war and were slow
to surrender to the Union even after General Robert
E. Lee and the rest of the Confederacy's soldiers laid
down their weapons. Standhope Uwatie, a Cherokee
Confederate brigadier general and commander of the
Confederate Indian cavalry, was the last rebel commander to lay down arms on June 23, 1865. Even after
that, the Indian rebels continued to fight for months;
braves raided Union camps in Oklahoma every few
weeks, and Indian slaveholders defied federal law and
continued to hold African Americans as slaves. Their
resistance was born out of their attachment to the institution of slavery and their hatred of the US government.

Indians in the southern states began enslaving
African Americans as early as the eighteenth century,
after they were introduced to the practice by white set-
tlers. For some Indians, such as the Creek and the Paw-
nee, holding slaves had been a part of their culture before
their first contact with Europeans; for the majority, however, their entanglement with slavery began when they
became the first victims of it. In the colonies of Georgia,
Mississippi, Florida, and Alabama, Indians were held as
slaves alongside African Americans. Later, as the practice
of enslaving Indians declined in the early 1800s, members of the Creek, Choctaw, Cherokee, Seminole, and
Chickasaw tribes began to show up at slave auctions to
purchase trafficked African Americans. As they shifted
from pelt hunting to farming as their main source of
income, plantation slavery became normal in Indian

communities. In the 1830s and '40s, Indians were displaced from the South by President Andrew Jackson's Indian removal policy. Federal troops removed tens of thousands of Cherokee, Creek, Seminole, Chickasaw, and Choctaw Indians, forcing them to relocate to Oklahoma. They traveled on foot, in stagecoaches, or on the backs of horses across the Mississippi, taking their slaves with them into the wilderness. At the end of the journey, they reached an undeveloped patch of land that the government called the Indian Territory. The Indians translated the name into Choctaw and called their new home Okla Humma, meaning "land of the red people."

The area was also home to the thousands of African Americans who made the journey as slaves to the new region. On the journey, migrants battled heat waves and hurricanes. They fought outbreaks of whooping cough, typhus, dysentery, and cholera, all the while being given inadequate rations of food and water by the federal troops who chaperoned their removal from their homelands. The African American slaves who made the journey, sometimes in chains, were assigned the bulk of the manual labor and were often the last to receive a bite of food or sip of water. As a result, they had the highest mortality rate during the already deadly trip. For the Indians and African Americans who survived the march, it would come to be known among them as the Trail of Tears.

Three decades later, when the Civil War began, the five tribes of Oklahoma pledged allegiance to the Confederacy. They joined the rebels to defend their rights as slaveholders and exact revenge on the federal government. During the Civil War, the Confederacy failed to send weapons or reinforcements to Oklahoma. As a result, the Indian rebels in Oklahoma were massacred when they had to do battle with Union fighters. Nonetheless, at the war's end, they refused to surrender. Late in 1865, under threat of all-out war, the leaders of each tribe were summoned to Reconstruction conferences in Arkansas and Washington, D.C., to negotiate their terms of surrender. First, the government demanded that the surrendering tribes sign a new peace treaty with the US government. Second, they were to emancipate their slaves and give them tribal rights. Last, they were to cede roughly a quarter of their land as reparations to the federal government for having joined the Confederacy.

The terms of the surrender of the Indians in Oklahoma brought jubilation and hope to the African Americans who had been their slaves. Slowly, at the end of 1865, more than five thousand enslaved African Americans in the territory were set free. Upon Emancipation, they began to advocate that the confiscated Indian land be broken up into 40- or 160-acre parcels and given to them to start farms. Some even dreamed that the ceded Indian territory could be turned into an all-black state. All over the country emancipated African Americans and their allies, the Union Army and the Radical Republicans in Congress, advocated that African Americans be given 40 acres of land, perhaps with a mule and a plow.

In Oklahoma, the realization of those hopes felt attainable. African Americans dreamed they could build a promised land on the old Indian lands, a place of their own where they could achieve economic independence as self-employed farmers. In anticipation, hundreds of African American families took up residence on the Indian lands, living in shantytowns made up of old slave quarters and canvas tents.

Almost as soon as they began squatting on the ceded Indian land, bands of Choctaw and Chickasaw Indians with war paint smeared on their cheeks and carrying whips began riding into the encampments on random nights, raiding and pillaging homes. They looted and smashed and dragged black men out of their homes to publicly whip or lynch them as women and children watched. Despite those intimidations, the dreamers in Oklahoma remained, hoping that any day the government would give them the right to petition to be given the land.

In 1866, after the Indian tribes of Oklahoma finalized their surrender with a transfer of more than 5 million acres in the center of the Indian Territory to the federal government, African Americans began to petition the Bureau of Land Management for parcels of land. Under the Homestead Act passed by Abraham Lincoln in 1862, Americans could petition the government for an allotment of publicly held lands. Soon after the first inquiries were received, the Bureau of Land Management rejected them announcing that the lands had already been earmarked as a resettlement territory for a new group of Indians who were being removed from the Midwest on the second Trail of Tears. Defeated, some African Americans stayed and fought to be accepted as tribesmen by the Indians who had once held them as slaves; others left Oklahoma altogether to find their way elsewhere in the emancipated world. There would be no 40 acres for them; there would be no promised land. Not yet.

7

Bob Church Versus Jim Crow

1862

MEMPHIS, TENNESSEE

After he swam to freedom in the Mississippi and emerged on the shore of the Union-occupied town of Memphis, Robert Reed Church was first finally a free man, but he also faced starting life over on land. He had a small savings from tips he earned on the boat, but no friends or allies to speak of in town. He decided to seek out his best possible lifeline: his father, Captain Church. He showed up on his father's doorstep, and Captain Church invited him in. They retreated to the parlor, sat together in armchairs, and talked. Captain Church expressed regret for having turned Robert over to the Confederacy. "I had no choice," he told him. Robert forgave the captain, who agreed to do what he could to back him in his endeavors in Memphis—without, of course, openly acknowledging that they were father and son.

In his first days as a free man in Memphis, Robert also met a woman named Louisa "Lou" Ayers. She was a former house slave for a prominent white Memphis family and had remained as a servant with them after the Union forces had arrived. Lou had been provided with an education while she was in their service and could read, write, and speak a few words of French. She was seventeen with soft features, skin the color of sand, loosely curled hair pinned in an updo, and deep-set eyes. She was best known for her laugh, which was lilting and infectious and charmed everyone she met, including Robert.

Robert lacked Lou's formal education and genteel manner. To most who encountered him, he was gruff and spartan, betraying his upbringing as a riverboat slave. Often he spoke only when spoken to and lapsed into broken English. In social situations, however, he was convivial, telling stories and chatting about current events, channeling the southern charms of his father and the businessmen on his boats.

He began to call on Lou often after they met and thought about asking for her hand in marriage. As he was falling in love with her, however, he was nagged by thoughts of his slave wife, Margaret Pico, and their daughter, Laura Church, in New Orleans. In Memphis there was peace, as the colored troops of the Union held control of the city, but elsewhere the Civil War made much of the South a dangerous battlefront, and there

was no way he could get to them. He and Lou were falling for each other; perhaps, he thought, the best thing
to do would be to move on from Margaret. A few months
after they met, he asked Lou to be his wife.

Robert and Lou married in Memphis in 1863, in
front of friends of the family, in the yard of a mansion
that belonged to the family that owned her. Captain
Church attended, and the family that owned Lou purchased her an expensive wedding dress from New York
City. A few months after they were married, Lou gave
birth to a daughter on September 23, 1863, the day
after Abraham Lincoln issued the Emancipation Proc-
lamation. They named her Mary Church, after Captain
Church's wife and daughter.

After Robert became a father for the second time,
he was eager to introduce his daughter to his father. He
traveled across town to his father's estate. In Captain
Church's parlor, the old ship commander bounced
Robert's daughter Mary on his knee. "You've got a good
girl here, Bob," he told him. "You have to make sure to
raise her right." Captain Church was proud of Robert
even if he did not say it aloud. The two shared a bond
that could not be openly spoken of; it would be years before Robert would reveal to his own child that Captain
Church, his former owner, was her grandfather.

IN 1866, AFTER THE WAR ENDED AND AFRICAN AMERICANS WERE
emancipated, Robert traveled to New Orleans to see

Margaret Pico and seven-year-old Laura in New Orleans. When he found his former wife, she was married to another man and had given Laura her new husband's surname: Napier. Robert requested that he be allowed to take Laura to Memphis, where he would pay for her to be put in school. A year later he sent for Laura and had her brought up to Memphis via steamboat. In Tennessee, she lived with Robert, Lou, and Mary and changed her name to Laura Church.

In the months after Emancipation, the Union troops stayed in town to keep the peace. The town was full of Confederate luminaries such as Nathan Bedford Forrest and the ex–Confederate president Jefferson Davis, as well as a population of former slaves. Its streets, made of wood planks, creaked as they were patrolled by a police force made of Confederate veterans; the local government was dominated by rebel-sympathizing Democrats. In many towns in the South, including the Memphis Union brigades, colored troops were left in place to protect the free black population after slavery ended. However, the troops' presence stirred resentment in the ex-Confederates in those towns, who felt they were being occupied by Northern emissaries of the federal government.

The Union troops in Memphis were mostly black men, many of them former slaves. During the day, they patrolled the streets and kept order, to the chagrin of many whites in town, especially the police force. At night the colored troops enjoyed drinking and carousing in parlors and brothels. Robert, who had come of age working in the parlors of Captain Church's ships, saw a business opportunity. With a loan from his wife, who had opened a successful wig shop, he started a billiard hall. In 1866, he applied for a business license but was denied on the basis of his color. To hell with them, he thought, and set up his business without the paperwork. His billiard hall was in a storefront on Gayoso Street just off Second Avenue near the riverfront. Inside, he set up pool tables, a bar stocked with whiskey, and a cash register. In an adjacent room, he built a ballroom where he threw soirees and dances attended by locals, which on occasion devolved into brawls that spilled out into the street.

One night, two white police officers showed up at Church's Billiard Hall and arrested him for operating a billiard hall without a license. Robert hired a lawyer and the case went to trial in April 1866, just days after Congress passed the Civil Rights Act. The Civil Rights Act was passed by the Radical Republican caucus in Congress, overriding a presidential veto of Andrew Jackson. It declared that all persons born in the United States were citizens and entitled to equal treatment under the law. On April 17, the charges against Church were dropped. Confederates in Memphis saw his victory as an affirmation of the Radical Republicans' Civil Rights Act. He swaggered away from the courtroom a free man but also a marked one. The events occurred against a backdrop of escalating racial tensions in Memphis, making

Church a hero among blacks and a villain among the ex-Confederate white population.

In Memphis, an uneasy peace existed between the races. It was shattered by free black men taking a liberty that the ex-Confederates could not stomach: having sex with white women. A riot began with a quarrel between the Memphis police and black Union soldiers outside a brothel by the riverfront, where black Union troops were known to bed white prostitutes. The scrum escalated, and several of the Union troops were gunned down. The Memphis police then went on a murderous crawl through the city, shooting black men and white northern carpetbaggers and raping black women. As the riots raged on, word reached Robert that the mob was looking for him. They wanted to kill the black man who had opened a business in spite of the state and then used the Civil Rights Act to get off scot-free. As Robert dressed that day, Lou, pregnant with their second child, begged him to remain home for fear he'd be killed. He slicked his black hair, goatee, and mustache straight with oil and put on his jacket. "No," he told her. He was not going to hide.

He showed up at his billiard hall and opened shop. He stayed until nightfall, but hardly anyone showed up. Still he refused to close up. He wasn't hoping to avoid the white mob, he was waiting for them. "Never be a coward," Captain Church had taught him. It had just begun to rain when the group of men finally showed up. "Get out here!" the men standing outside wearing police uniforms and holding guns yelled. David Roach, an Irish police officer, told Robert to close up the hall. Robert went back in the shop, turning his back on the men. He heard the crash of shattering glass as bullets started to ring out. He then heard a pop and felt a burning in the back of his neck. It took him a moment to realize he'd been shot. The men stormed the store as Church lay on the floor, bleeding from the head. They drank from the bottles and barrels of whiskey at the bar. They removed several hundred dollars from the cash register. They broke his pool tables. Finally they left him for dead and put a torch to his building with him inside. The rain slowed the flames as they engulfed the store, and somehow Robert dragged himself from the burning building, half dead with a bullet wound in his head. He had escaped possible death for the third time.

NO ONE IN TOWN HEARD FROM ROBERT IN THE AFTERMATH OF the riots. Was he dead? Had he run? A bipartisan consort of congressmen led by the Radical Republican Elihu Washburne arrived in town from Washington, D.C., to conduct an investigation of the riots. They interviewed black Tennesseans, local government officials, and the police officers involved in the riot. Toward the end, a man with a wound on his head came ambling up to speak with the congressmen. He introduced himself as Robert Reed Church.

"How much of a colored man are you?" Washburne asked. He, perhaps, was shocked that the rioters had attacked a man who looked so white.

"I do not know, very little. My father was a white man. My mother was as white as I am."

Robert told his story of being shot and lying bleeding as the rioters had ransacked his store. He named his assailant as Officer Dave Roach, adding, "He is down at the tavern right now." After the investigation, the federal government opted not to bring any charges as a result of the riots and most of the policemen kept their jobs. Forty-six black people were killed; five black women raped; seventy-five people, including Robert, injured; over a hundred were robbed; ninety-one homes, twelve black schools, and five black churches burned; and $100,000 ($1.6 million) of property damage was done. "We have decided this does not merit federal charges," the investigators concluded.

In the aftermath of the riot and the government's inaction in dealing with its perpetrators, thousands left Memphis, but thousands more stayed, refusing to give in to mob terror. Among them was Robert Reed Church. As merchants closed their stores and families left their homes, Church began buying real estate. He purchased five properties in what was coming to be known as the Beale Street District. In 1867, months after having nearly died, Robert became a father again, this time to a son, whom he and Lou named Thomas. With his family and business portfolio growing in Memphis,

Robert was resolute about staying and helping to rebuild the city. The Beale Street District was the heart of black Memphis. After the riots those in the African American community who remained flowed into the southern tip of Memphis, a district extending from the riverfront for eleven blocks into the city. Its dirt streets held an office of the Freedmen's Bureau, a black church, black rooming houses, brick stores and bars, and wood-frame houses. In Beale, the African American community built a stronghold after the riots, dancing to the music of traveling black brass bands in saloons and dressing in their best clothes to attend church. Following Sunday church service, men still dressed in suits with gold and silver watch chains hanging from the pockets congregated on corners to socialize, laugh, and make small talk. The throngs of black people on the streets were a constant source of complaint for white women who had to cross through the district to run errands.

One Sunday afternoon, Robert was standing on a street corner talking with a group of men. A police officer approached the men and told them to disperse. When they didn't comply, he grabbed Robert by his collar. Robert wrestled free, drew his gun from his hip, and fired a warning shot over the officer's head. The officer then pulled his gun, pistol-whipped Church over the head, and dragged him off to jail. Church hired a lawyer and evaded any formal charges.

The white rioters had burned Church's billiard hall to the ground the night they had shot him, but in 1870 it was rebuilt. He leased a two-story brick building on

Beale Street. The first floor held a bar in its main room, laid out much like the parlors in his father's ship. The bar was stocked with liquors, fine wines, and expensive cigars. The next room held a billiard hall with new pool tables. In a third room was a barbershop with its own entrance. Outside the building was a watermelon stand where a boy Church employed called out, "Watermelon, watermelon!" luring foot traffic toward Church's corner. Over each entrance was a black sign lettered with gold leaf that read R. R. CHURCH.

ONE WINTER A FEW YEARS LATER, IT SNOWED IN MEMPHIS FOR THE first time in memory. A snowfall in the Mississippi delta was unexpected, but Robert Reed Church had foreseen such an event and was prepared for the occasion. In a previous year, on a trip up North, he had purchased a sleigh. His friends had made fun of him, thinking he was insane to have brought a sled back to Memphis, a hot, muggy city year-round. Robert predicted that "one day it will snow here" and he would have an opportunity to use it. "You'll see," he told them. When the snow finally did come, he affixed it to his horse and rode around town with his young daughter Mary next to him. As they glided through the streets of Memphis, pulled by a galloping steed, they watched as people on the sidewalks and in their yards played in the snow and tossed snowballs at one another. At one point he was struck by a hail of snow-balls and laughed, thinking it to be good-natured fun. But when he picked up one of the snowballs, he found that it was a rock covered in snow. A larger rock then came hurling at him and hit him in the face. Robert pulled out the revolver he kept at his side and pointed it at the men who had thrown the rock. He let off a shot, and they scattered. Robert drove the sled home. "My father had the most violent temper of any man I ever met," his daughter recalled.

Church saloons were a constant center of police activity. On many nights, his bars were the sites of brawls, shootings, and stabbings. In the late 1860s, his old friend from the docks Blanche K. Bruce walked into his bar. Since Emancipation he had become one of the wealthiest black men in Mississippi, having purchased a large sharecropping plantation there. He was weigh-ing a run for the US Senate and wanted to know what Church, a black man of similar background and status, thought of the idea. If elected, he would be the second-ever black senator. Church advised Bruce to run. "I'll support you," he assured him. After Bruce announced his candidacy, he returned to Church's saloon several times to raise money or talk strategy with him. In 1875, he was elected to the Senate from Mississippi. After Bruce's election and with his own money, celebrity, and political connections, Church became a political power broker seemingly overnight. Their rough-and-tumble environment aside, his saloons also served as de facto headquarters for black political and civil rights activity. Aspiring black politicians would wade through a crowd of gamblers and partiers to talk to him. Local Republicans would often visit his bar to ask for an endorsement or advice. His burgeoning political machine was mockingly called *'de 'siety* by white racists, who doubted that Church and his friends, as black men, had the ability to make any political impact.

Church and his band of black political mavens would face an uphill battle. In 1877, the remainder of the Union forces in Memphis left the city when the newly elected president, Rutherford B. Hayes, decreed that he was returning the South to "home rule." Hayes ordered away the Union troops that had protected blacks and their white Republican allies in the South. Almost immediately ex-Confederates returned to power, as the constituents of an antiblack Democratic party, eager to reverse a decade of racial progress.

⌇

THE SUMMER OF 1878 WAS MUGGY AND HOT AND BESET BY SWARMS of mosquitoes. On the first day of August, a steamboat worker who had slipped out of a yellow fever quarantine in Vicksburg, Mississippi, sat down to eat in a restaurant by the docks operated by a woman named Kate Bionda. He infected Bionda, who died just over two weeks later, but not before infecting numerous others and beginning a yellow fever outbreak in Memphis. The infection often resulted in the vomiting of blood and the developing of jaundice, which gave the eyes and skin of the infected a yellow hue. It spread quickly and could kill within a few weeks. In Memphis, the epidemic exploded with more than a thousand infections and two hundred deaths within its first few weeks.

When Robert heard of the first cases, he rushed home and packed all his children's things into a trunk. He then took Thomas, eleven, and Mary, fifteen, to the train station. At the station, people who were departing were weeping, as were those they abandoned. "You are leaving us poor folks behind," a voice shouted from the crowds. "But you better watch out. Death can find you where you are going just as easy as it can find us here with yellow fever."

Church's father also left Memphis during the outbreak. He moved to Monmouth, Arkansas, with his wife and daughter to receive medical treatments for rheumatism and perhaps escape the possibility of catching the fever. Robert couldn't give too much thought to his father's departure; he was much more concerned with the fate of his children and his loved ones who remained in Memphis. Shortly after arriving in Arkansas, however, Captain Church died of a brain aneurysm.

Church barely had time to grieve as the outbreak worsened and the death toll rose. As he walked to his saloon every day he saw bodies lining the streets. Each day as he worked he heard funeral bells chiming nearly every hour as deaths mounted to more than two hundred a week. Just as blacks had fled Memphis after the race riots, whites fled Memphis in even larger numbers during the outbreak, leaving behind whites without the means to relocate and the majority of the African American population. As the outbreak wore on, African Americans who were infected with yellow fever died at a lower rate than whites, perhaps due to a resistance developed by African Americans from increased exposure to yellow fever during slavery.

One day, while he was walking the streets, he lifted up one of the rickety wood planks that was used to pave the roads, as something told him to take a closer look. When he peeled up the rotted wood, he found a pool of filthy foul-smelling water. He theorized that the unsanitary condition of the streets had to be responsible for the spread of sickness. He came to believe that once the streets were paved over, the yellow fever epidemic would subside. The pools of water under the streets were indeed the culprit, as they served as the breeding grounds for mosquitoes, which scientists would later learn were the vector for the yellow fever virus.

Church followed through on his hunch by buying up houses for pennies on the dollar from families fleeing Memphis and became a large-scale property owner in the city, knowing that if the city rebounded after the fever, he would become rich. He also increased his purchase order for whiskey, which he sold as an antiseptic during the worst days of the plague.

In 1879, when the epidemic began to abate, the city of Memphis emerged bankrupt. After years of people and businesses fleeing, the city was out of money. In order to pay down its debts, the local government issued bonds. The first bond was sold for $1,000 ($27,092) to Robert Reed Church.

To the surprise of many, Memphis' most hated black citizen was the first to step up to try to save the city. After his bond purchase, other prominent local businessmen and families followed suit. Church's actions helped Memphis survive the outbreak and rebuild after it, garnering him goodwill from Memphis' white citizens and solidifying his reputation as the city's most prominent black son. Meanwhile, the money from the bonds was used to rebuild Memphis, and as one of the city's largest property owners Church stood to make a hefty sum from the redevelopment.

8

Mother of Civil Rights in California

Mary Ellen Pleasant and JJ returned to San Francisco after John Brown was executed in December 1859. "Brown was an earnest, sincere man and as brave a man as ever lived, but he lacked judgment and was sometimes foolhardy," she lamented. In California, she and JJ regrouped. Her funds were depleted by more than $40,000 ($976,000), principally from her investment in Brown's insurrection. Pleasant had staked so much on Harpers Ferry. However, she would not entertain the thought that it had been a mistake. "I never regretted the times or the money I spent on the idea," she said.

Pleasant took a job as a domestic servant for a wealthy San Francisco industrialist named Selim Woodworth. He lived in a mansion high up in the city's hills, with dozens of rooms and a view of the bay. After hiring Pleasant, he moved both her and JJ into his home. As the house manager, Pleasant supervised his staff of maids, chauffeurs, butlers, and cooks, and assisted his young wife, Lisette, in looking after the couple's children and large extended family who lived at the house, including Selim's elderly grandmother.

Pleasant threw herself into the work. It was just a few months ago that she believed she would be helping John Brown lead a slave revolt and govern a free black colony. Now she was working as the help. Pleasant's arrangement allowed her to get back on her feet and make up some of her monetary losses. Head domestics in San Francisco were paid handsomely—upward of $200 a month ($5,423)—and were provided room and board. Pleasant was not one to let her pride get in the way of making progress.

The bright spot in her new role was Selim's wife. Lisette was in her twenties and young enough to be Pleasant's daughter. Lisette was blond with a slight frame, and tiny compared to the towering Pleasant. The two quickly became friends, and spent the days walking the hallways, leaning on each other, and supervising the staff. Lisette sometimes affectionately referred to Pleasant as "mama."

⌐⥳⌐

A LITTLE OVER A YEAR AFTER PLEASANT RETURNED TO CALIFORnia, Abraham Lincoln was elected president and soon after the Civil War began. Pleasant was gladdened. "[My work with Brown] seemed at first like a failure, but time proved that the money was well spent," she said. "It paved the way for the war." Woodworth had to leave home when he was ordered to return to the navy to command a gunboat, the USS *John P. Jackson*, as part of a fleet detached to the Mississippi River to sink Confederate ships and help conquer the Mississippi ports. Perhaps in gratitude for his hospitality, Pleasant decided to remain at the Woodworths' during the war and look after the household. There she continued to manage the house and help his young wife with the family. When the war ended and Selim returned home, Pleasant and JJ moved out. Afterward, Pleasant and Lisette remained close and Pleasant stopped by the house frequently to help her run the house.

Just after the war ended Pleasant made a splash on San Francisco's social scene, when she threw a wedding for her daughter, Lizzie, who had moved from the East. Lizzie had fallen for a businessman named R. B. Phillips. The wedding was covered by San Francisco's black newspaper, *The Elevator*, which called the affair splendid entertainment. The expensively fashioned gala was the first public display of Pleasant's wealth and the beginning of her embracing a more public profile.

DURING THE RECONSTRUCTION YEARS IN SAN FRANCISCO, PLEASant entered a new phase in which she took a higher profile in both her business and activist efforts. As African

Americans readied to fight for their rights, black San Francisco was dealt a blow in 1862, when the California courts awarded the land of the black millionaire William Leidesdorff to the estate of Joseph Folsom, a white industrialist who swindled him out of the land. Chief among the concerns of African Americans in San Francisco after the war was the desegregation of San Francisco's streetcars. The cars, which provided fast and affordable transport, were off-limits to blacks. The drivers were instructed not to stop for African Americans and not to let them board. Pleasant made it her mission to desegregate the streetcars.

To do so she devised a plan to catch the streetcar companies in the act of discriminating, in violation of the freshly minted Civil Rights Act of 1866, and then file suit against them. She began with the Omnibus Railroad & Cable Company, which served the southern part of San Francisco, where many African Americans lived. One afternoon in 1866, she waited on a street corner as a streetcar approached, pulled down the track by horses. When the car stopped, Pleasant got on but was told by the driver to get off. She stepped off the car and later that day filed a lawsuit. Before the case could reach court, the streetcar company contacted Pleasant to make a settlement with her. Pleasant dropped the suit in exchange for Omnibus' agreeing to allow African Americans to ride its cars. But even after she withdrew her claim, she wasn't finished; she was going to go after San Francisco's other big rail company.

Pleasant decided to try to catch the North Beach and Mission Railroad Company in the act of discrimination. The NBMRR was a much bigger company that served the wealthy neighborhoods in the north of San Francisco. They would not give in as easily as Omnibus, so Pleasant had to lay her trap precisely. She enlisted the help of Lisette Woodworth, the matriarch of one of the city's most respected white families. Everything went as planned: on September 27, 1866, they met near Lisette's house, and Lisette boarded the car one stop before Pleasant. When the streetcar approached Pleasant, she flailed her arms to try to get the driver to stop. The driver looked at her but kept driving. Afterward, Pleasant hired a high-priced attorney named George W. Tyler and sued. The lawyer filed a suit in late 1866 or early 1867 charging that "the agents and servants of the defendant (NBMRR) acted under instructions received from said defendant requiring them to refuse to stop the cars of said defendant to allow 'colored people' or people of African Descent, to get on board." He added that she had "suffered greatly in her mind" and furthermore "was compelled to and did proceed on foot to her destination, not being at the time in a physical condition to do so, causing thereby great suffering of body." Lisette testified that she had been on the car when it had bypassed Pleasant.

ON THE DAY HER CASE WAS HEARD IN COURT, PLEASANT, GEORGE Tyler, and Lisette arrived at the court thronged by reporters.

Inside the courtroom, Pleasant and NBMRR's lawyers made their arguments. Finally, Pleasant's star witness, Lisette Woodworth, took the stand.

"Can you describe the circumstances of the NBMRR incident?" George Tyler asked.

"I was in the car when she hailed it. I saw her hail it, and the conductor took no notice of her and walked into the car," Woodsworth began. "Said I to the conductor, 'Stop this car; there is a woman who wants to get in.' His answer was, 'We don't take colored people in the cars.' I then said, 'You will have to let me out.'"

"How long have you known Mrs. Pleasant?"

"Ten years," she replied. "I know her well enough that I call her 'Mamma' sometimes."

The court decided in Pleasant's favor and declared that NBMRR had discriminated against her on the basis of her race. The courts ordered NBMRR to desegregate its cars and awarded Pleasant $500 ($6,863) in damages. It was a landmark victory.[*] The win was celebrated all over San Francisco by African Americans with rounds of beer and cigars.

During the Civil War, the California law that banned blacks from testifying in court was revised by the state legislature to award blacks' testimony rights. When Pleasant took the stand in her suit, it was the first prominent court case in California in which an African American could

---

[*] *Mary E. Pleasants v. NBMRR* set the precedent for future desegregation cases. It also happened to pave the way for Maya Angelou to become San Francisco's first black streetcar conductor in 1944.

testify, to the chagrin of those in the state who were angry about the growing role of minorities in California.

In 1867, as Pleasant's case was being decided, Californians in a backlash elected a white supremacist Democrat, Henry Huntly Haight, as governor.

The white newspapers downplayed Pleasant's victory and instead focused on Lisette's comment that she knew Pleasant well enough to call her "Mamma." The papers nicknamed Pleasant "Mammy Pleasant," invoking the racist stereotype of the plantation mammy. Pleasant was from the North and had never lived on a plantation; nonetheless, the name stuck.* "When certain newspapers tried to slacken my character, I thought to myself, they must have some money to pay their hands with, and if they can get a dollar for abusing me, it helped maintain printers' wages and kept more people at work, and I like to see people employed," she later stated.

For racists in San Francisco, Pleasant's desegregating their streetcars was only the latest blow. After the Civil War, Chinese immigrants had begun migrating to California in large numbers to work in the mines and open laundries. Their presence was met with anger by many among California's mostly white population. In

---

* The assertions that Pleasant was a former slave, a mammy, a Voodoo priestess, or a madame are apocryphal. They are based almost solely on the accounts of Charlotte Dennis Downs, the daughter of one of Pleasant's employees, whom Pleasant did not know well. Downs claimed that Pleasant had dictated her "true" memoirs to her in the 1880s. Downs was never able to produce the manuscript, claiming she lost it.

retaliation, anti-Chinese laws were passed, including a tax on the wages of foreign miners, and the San Francisco police adopted a policy of ignoring crimes if the victims were Chinese or Indian, leading to a massacre of Indians in 1870 and a mass lynching of Chinese immigrants in 1871.

After she won in court, Pleasant purchased a mansion in downtown San Francisco and began making renovations to turn it into a boardinghouse. The house was built of dark-colored stone and rose three stories with dozens of rooms, a parlor, and a formal dining room. The property was located within walking distance of city hall, the banking district, and the opera house, making it a prime choice of lodging for the city's rich bachelors. She outfitted the house with imported armchairs and chaises, velvet drapes, and fine art. "It was the leading boardinghouse in San Francisco and set the best table," she bragged. "Many of the best families of the city lived with me." She put up politicians, bankers, and industrialists at the home, serving them five-course meals she herself prepared and charming them with elegant soirees that she threw in the ballroom of the house. Her boardinghouse was popular with men from the South. "Southerners love niggers," she commented.

In her first year of operation, she boarded six tenants and charged them a little over $300 ($5,000) a month; she made $15,000 ($300,000) in profit her first year. She also opened two laundries to offer cleaning services to her boarders and add another source

of income. Her laundries were set up in the backs
of stores. Inside, African American men and women
she hired dredged soiled garments on wooden wash-
ing boards in metal tubs of frothy water. The laundry
business met a huge demand. It was common to see
even wealthy men walking the streets of San Francisco
with brown tobacco and coffee stains on their shirts.
Those who did have their clothes laundered did so by
having them shipped off to China or the Sandwich Islands (Hawaii), where they would be laundered and
returned on cargo vessels, a process that was prohibi-
tively expensive—upward of $25 ($600) for a dozen
shirts—and painfully slow. Many chose to wear their
soiled garments instead. Early laundries in California
such as Pleasant's charged as much as $5 ($136) for a
dozen shirts and made upward of $4,000 ($80,000) a
year in profits, making a laundry a surprisingly good
investment.

IN 1870, PLEASANT TOOK IN A POLITICIAN AND MERCHANT NAMED
Newton Booth as a boarder. Booth was tall with a slight
build that would have made him look frail had it not
been for his broad chest and shoulders. He had a serious
face with a thick goatee and mustache and heavy-lidded
eyes. His dark hair was receding, and he kept it slicked
back. He was an intellectual and seemed to always be
deep in contemplation. In Pleasant's parlor, he mused
about the future of America, praising the charity of the

rich and the innovation of its inventors, while lamenting that greed was causing the fruits of its prosperity to be distributed unequally. Pleasant was smitten with Booth. "I consider him to be the greatest intellect California ever produced," she said.

While boarding with Pleasant, Booth decided to run for governor of California against the Democratic incumbent, Henry Huntly Haight. Setting out from Pleasant's house, he canvassed the state, spreading his visions of economic fairness and societal improvement. "It is strange that, in a country where there are hundreds of millions of acres of unsettled land; in an age when mechanical inventions have tenfold increased the power of production, daily bread and comfortable homes should not be easily within the reach of all," he declared. His speeches resonated with a population that had largely missed the prosperity of the gold and silver rushes and watched barons build mansions in the hills, while they struggled to get by. In 1871, Booth won the election.

After his victory, Pleasant threw Booth a celebration party at her house. She hired musicians and prepared a gourmet feast with champagne toasts for the occasion. Pleasant and Booth made a grand entrance together, arriving in Pleasant's horse-drawn carriage. They emerged from the carriage arm in arm and entered the party together. When Pleasant greeted her guests, she held Booth by the elbow, telling them, with a wide grin, "This is Governor Booth, who has been elected from my house."

As Pleasant's prospects were soaring, JJ fell ill. He was diagnosed with diabetes, which at the time was a terminal illness. The disease was still a mystery to doctors, and there were no treatments available other than special diets, which had varying effectiveness. Some doctors recommended fasting, others a diet of all meat and dairy products or all oatmeal. At best those special diets could delay death by only a few years.

Pleasant's streetcar case and her friendship with the new governor in California brought her fame within San Francisco's small African American community. African Americans began to seek her out for help at her boardinghouse on Washington Street. Her kitchen took up almost the entire back half of the house. Inside she had three ovens that she kept stuffed with turkeys, ducks, and cakes. Dozens of workers, preparing legs of ham, kneading dough for bread, and mixing cake batter buzzed around her. Visitors entered the kitchen through a back door, where she took deliveries of beer and dry goods. Many came to ask for help. Pleasant was known among African Americans and women in San Francisco as a woman who could get things done. She had the money and connections to solve most problems and opened her kitchen to those seeking aid. Her kitchen came to be known in San Francisco as "Black City Hall." Some needed money, others housing, or a job. Women of all races came seeking help finding a husband or getting a divorce. Once she finished preparing dinner, she would go to work to find those who came for help what they needed.

IN THE EARLY 1870S PLEASANT BEGAN CONSTRUCTION ON A MAN-sion. It sat on a two-acre lot on a hill in a well-to-do section of the city, west of the financial district, at 1660 Octavia Street. The main house of the estate was designed in an Italian style, with a low-pitched roof and a white-stone exterior. The back of the house had views of the bay and a winding staircase that climbed three floors and led to more than thirty rooms.

The hub of the house was the kitchen. It now became the new "Black City Hall." There she received emancipated slaves who had migrated to San Francisco, trained them as domestics, and placed them in jobs. She counseled young women and African Americans who were in legal trouble and gave them money for legal fees. She also provided start-up capital for African Americans who wanted to start businesses. Pleasant gave the loans in exchange for collecting a monthly cash royalty, adding even more streams of revenue from other saloons, laundries, and boardinghouses. When the mansion was completed, Pleasant took in an acquaintance, Thomas Bell, as a boarder. He was the director of two railroad companies, one in Nevada and one in California. He was a trustee in the Union Mill and Mining Company and a director of the Bank of California. Bell was a Scotsman; he had dark hair that was thinning on the top, a long, straight nose, and a thick mustache that drooped over his lips.

Bell and Pleasant began investing their money together after he moved into her home. They bought up stock in Nevada mining companies. Their bet paid dividends when Nevada entered a silver boom, after large deposits of silver were found in the state's mountains. Their profits from these investments made Bell even richer, and made Pleasant a millionaire in her own right. The two entrepreneurs kept the equity details of their investment between them. However, their close relationship, cohabitation, and secrecy created speculation that they were not just partners but lovers.

To deter the rumors, that year Pleasant set up Bell with a wife. Bell was fifty-three years old and was sharing a bachelor pad with another millionaire in San Francisco. He had several illegitimate children and was a reputed womanizer. Pleasant introduced him to a friend of hers, a young woman from Massachusetts named Teresa Clingan. The two were married within months of their meeting. Pleasant planned and catered the wedding.

Shortly after the Bells' wedding, JJ passed away from diabetes. His death was followed by Lizzie's, who died suddenly, reportedly from alcohol abuse. Inside her mansion, Pleasant found herself widowed again. After their nuptials, the Bells moved into her house as a couple. Pleasant befriended Bell's younger wife as she had Lisette Woodworth. With JJ gone, it seemed the Bells were all she had now.

9

Saint or Sinner?

Late in the afternoon of July 29, 1885, a hot day, Robert Reed Church was at work behind the bar in his pool hall when he smelled smoke. He was now forty-six years old and wore a bowler hat to cover the wounds on his head he had sustained in the attack on his shop during the Memphis race riots almost twenty years before. He went outside and saw that the lumber factory up the street was on fire and that the flames were moving in his direction. He didn't panic. Between the ship fire on the *Bulletin No. 2* he had survived as a teenager and being burned out during the race riots in his first days as a free man, he had lost his fear of fire. He yelled out for three of his employees and sent them to the roof with buckets of water and fire hoses. He then rallied the rest of his staff and customers and ordered them to start carrying the pool tables and furniture outside into the street.

By that time the fire had engulfed the entire block, and a panic ensued. Men and women evacuated their homes, dragging their possessions into the street. Shopkeepers emptied their stores, trying to move as much merchandise as they could outside. As Church had his place cleaned out, the sky turned black with smoke as the flames burned down the telephone poles on the sides of the road, snapping their wires. When the flames reached Church's billiard hall, a strong gust of wind weakened the fire. A few minutes later, firefighters arrived to put out the blaze. His billiard hall sustained no damage other than a scorched floor and burned curtains. The rest of the block wasn't so fortunate; the fire burned out dozens of homes and businesses, causing $125,000 ($3.3 million) of damage.

Just as he had during the yellow fever outbreak, Church used the disaster as an opportunity. He swooped in and bought dozens of burned-out homes. Added to his existing real estate holdings, he owned nearly half of downtown Memphis after the fire. He fixed the fire damage, renovated the properties, and rented them out. He spared no expense with his remodeling. He reappointed the wood-frame homes and rooming houses with turrets and cupolas and let them to African Americans at affordable rents. In doing so, he offered them an alternative to the slumlike conditions and high rents demanded by white landlords in the area. Church was a charitable landlord, often letting black tenants who fell on hard times go months without paying rent.

He was less public-spirited with his commercial holdings. Having control of a plurality of the commercial real estate in Memphis, he could set his own prices. He charged exorbitant rents in his commercial buildings and let them out to whoever could pay them. Many of his new tenants were gambling houses, saloons, concert halls, and brothels. The black enclave of Beale Street was transformed into a red-light district. Some would denigrate Robert for bringing bordellos and dance clubs to Memphis, even sinking as low as to call him a pimp. Whenever such accusations were brought to him he'd reply, "Whatever my tenants do in their property is their business." His billiard hall sat in the middle of a growing vice district. Church capitalized on the new traffic his tenants brought with their dives, strip shows, and brothels. The pool hall began to function as a casino, pawnshop, and moneylender. Inside, high-stakes card, dice, and billiard games took place in the parlor. From behind the bar, Church made high-interest loans and bought clothing, diamonds, and other jewelry for pennies on the dollar, handing back wads of cash neatly rolled and bound to those he made transactions with.

Church had between $50,000 and $100,000 in cash and an income of $50,000 a year from rents and his pool hall. With a net worth near $300,000 ($8 million) and growing rapidly, he was one of the richest black men in the United States. As he was expanding his empire, his marriage to Lou was falling apart.

Years earlier, he had suffered a second gunshot wound to the head and hadn't been the same since. In 1878, while in Arkansas, he had gotten into a fight with a white police officer who had accosted a female associate of his. During the fight, the officer had pulled his gun and shot him. He had survived but had begun using morphine to cope with the pain. The drugs turned his eyes red and worsened his already violent temper. In 1881, he lost his friend and kindred spirit from the slave days, Blanche K. Bruce. Bruce's death was followed by the passing of his little brother, James Wilson. Wilson and Church had been reunited after the Civil War, trading stories, perhaps over whiskey, of how it sickened them that they had been forced to work for the Confederacy. "It was the most humiliating experience of my life," Wilson told Church, barely able to contain his anger. Wilson passed without a wife or children; Church buried him on an empty plot of land he owned in Memphis.

With his father, brother, and Senator Bruce now dead, Church's ties to his time in enslavement had failed. His marriage to Lou, a former slave, crumbled. Church became angrier, more morphine-dependent, and sank deeper into the world of vice he was building on Beale Street.

In 1884, he divorced Lou and began courting Anna Wright, a well-known black Memphis educator. Wright carried herself with an aristocratic air and dressed in the latest fashions. Like many African Americans in the years after Emancipation, she was ashamed of her roots in slavery and claimed that her family had never been enslaved, but rather had been willing servants of white patrons. She encouraged Robert to whitewash his past as well and wouldn't stand any reference to his enslavement. Wright was twenty-nine, just a few years older than his daughter Mary Church. She had fair skin, curly hair, and angular features and proudly claimed to be as much Indian as she was negro. They were married at Anna's home on New Year's Day 1885. The newlyweds honeymooned in New Orleans, where they were hosted by P. B. S. Pinchback, the black former governor of Louisiana. After returning from their honeymoon, the new couple built a mansion on a two-acre lot that Robert had purchased during the yellow fever epidemic. The mansion was in the Queen Anne style, with fourteen rooms decorated with crystal chandeliers and frescoed walls. In the main parlor hung a picture of the sinking *Bulletin No. 2* that Church had commissioned. In the back of the estate were horse stables and servants' quarters.

Church's home was built on an undeveloped stretch of Memphis outside the city center. He hoped the construction of his new home would spur other African Americans to build homes nearby and develop a wealthy black enclave. To his chagrin, it was wealthy white families that began to build houses around him. Nonetheless, the Church mansion, the home of the richest black man in the South, became a meeting place for America's black elite. Pinchback and other black dignitaries stayed at the Church residence whenever they passed through Memphis. The grandeur of Church's house and the prominence of his visitors aroused the curiosity of his white neighbors. They would often think up some excuse to try to see the interior of the house. They would ring the doorbell and tell Mrs. Church they had "just come to see the new home." She dealt with such requests by refusing to show the white neighbors the house herself, instead dispatching a servant to the door and leaving the room. In the house Mrs. Church wore long silk blue gowns, which trailed behind her as she whisked out of the room.

Robert was a much more convivial host than his wife. When he had company, he took to the kitchen to make his specialty, boiled pampano, a fish from the Louisiana gulf he had eaten often on the river as a boy. He loved to cook for guests. Inside the house, which his wife had carefully outfitted with fine furniture and rugs, hung bunches of bananas from chandeliers, banisters, and cabinets, so one was always within his reach if he or his guests got hungry. In the backyard, he kept crates of live turkeys and chickens, whose crowing could be heard from the house. He ordered flour, oil, nuts, and fruits in bulk.

As Robert Reed Church's gambles in real estate and politics had borne fruit, making him the richest and most powerful man in Tennessee, a young Memphis-based journalist named Ida B. Wells published a thinly veiled critique of him in the *New York Freedman* in December 1885. She wondered if the richest black man in the South had sold his soul for riches. "All of us can not be millionaires," she wrote. ". . . What material benefit is a 'leader' if he does not, to some extent, devote his time, talent and wealth to the alleviation of the poverty and misery, and elevation of his own people?" Church went from slave to gun-toting black maverick to wealthy and connected real estate magnate. The question was, now that he finally had power, would he use it for the betterment of his people? Wells was determined to push him in the right direction.

Church knew of Ida B. Wells. She attended the local Baptist church and socialized in the same circles as his daughter Mary. He had begun collecting her press clippings after she had sued to desegregate the ladies' car on the Chesapeake and Ohio Railway's trains in Tennessee and become a minor hero among local blacks. He read her article, which criticized "black leaders," and put a blue *X* next to it with a pen, as was his habit with articles he found interesting.

IN THE SUMMER OF 1886, WELLS LEFT MEMPHIS TO TAKE A TEACHing job in Visalia, California. She immediately regretted the decision but had no money to get back. She wrote to Robert Reed Church to ask for a loan. "[I] wrote a letter to Mr. C asking the loan for 100 dollars," she wrote in her diary. "I told him that I wrote him because he was the only man of my race who could lend me that much money and wait for me to repay it." A month later, she received an envelope from Memphis with a check inside from R. R. Church. Wells bought a ticket to Memphis and left Visalia within the week.

When she arrived in Memphis, she sought out Church. When she found him, she thanked him and promised to repay the loan. "No," he told her glaring back at her with bloodshot eyes. She didn't protest; Church wasn't the type of man to quarrel with. "My gratitude for his kindly act and his trust in a girl he only knew by reputation warms my heart," she remembered.

After she returned to Memphis, Wells took a job writing for the *Weekly Baptist*. Church's loan did not dissuade her from challenging him in print. She chastised African Americans for patronizing the institutions of Beale Street and spending their money on tobacco and liquor. Nonetheless, she occasionally let her admiration for Church slip though. In a scathing critique of black politicians, she once wrote, "One wealthy man is worth more than 1000 politicians." After Church made her the loan, Ida remained in touch with him and became friendly with his daughter Mary. However, though Robert would continue to support Ida financially, he deemed her too controversial for his daughter to associate with openly and advised Mary to keep her distance.

In 1888, Ida began writing for the *Memphis Free Speech*, an African American paper with a larger circulation. She focused her writings for the paper on the lynchings of black men in the South, which were growing into an epidemic. Her writings were controversial.

In them she encouraged black men to take up arms against lynchers and posited that white women who accused black men of rape were doing so to cover up their willing trysts with them. Her writings became so controversial that the paper's owner, Reverend Taylor Nightingale, was run out of town, and Ida ended up taking over the paper. As Church tried to keep Mary, whom he fancied as a southern belle, away from Ida, his personal respect for her grew. In her, he saw a fearlessness that mirrored his own. She reminded him of the edicts laid down by his father, Captain Church: If they strike you, strike them back; never be a coward.

Perhaps influenced by Wells, Church began to transform Beale Street in the 1880s. In 1889, he built an eponymous hotel that took up an entire city block. The Church Hotel had large rooms, a parlor with chandeliers, Persian carpets, and an oyster bar. After the completion of the establishment, he continued to rent to bordellos, strip joints, and bars, but he also recruited black lawyers, dentists, doctors, and publishers to Beale Street. His effort civilized Beale Street during the day, when it was full of black businesses and professionals. After they shuttered their shops for the day and the sun went down, Beale returned to being a red-light district.

IN 1890, CHURCH HOSTED FREDERICK DOUGLASS. THE CIVIL rights activist had first become acquainted with the Churches through Mary, who had met Douglass when she had attended the 1880 presidential inauguration in Washington, D.C., as a guest of her father's late friend Senator Blanche K. Bruce. As Church and his family prepared for Douglass to arrive, Anna Church gave strict instructions to their young children, Annette Church and Robert Reed Church Jr. on how to comport themselves. Annette was afraid of elderly people, and Douglass was seventy years old. Mrs. Church gave her strict instructions not to touch him or comment on his looks. When Douglass arrived, she defied her parents by staring at his hair, which was white and long and hung down over his ears; and ogling his suit, which had long tails that went almost to the floor. As he came through the door, little Annette ran toward him and kissed him then turned to her mother, exclaiming, "He's got such big eyes, Mamma." Douglass gave a hearty laugh.

Coincidentally, while Douglass was in Memphis, he became acquainted with Ida B. Wells. After he left they began a correspondence and collaborated on civil rights protests, including a boycott of the 1895 Chicago World's Fair for excluding black exhibits. Ironically, the Churches defied the boycott and were one of the only high-profile black families to attend the fair.

AS WELLS PUBLISHED ARTICLE AFTER ARTICLE ABOUT SOUTHERN lynchings, she influenced Church, who at times appeared distant from the struggle for racial equality. It was perhaps a surprise when, in the late 1880s, he joined the Tennessee Rifles, a volunteer militia of black men formed to fight potential lynch mobs. In 1892, an African American man opened a grocery store in Memphis called the People's Grocery. The store was located just outside Memphis in a two-story brick storehouse and sold crates of fresh vegetables and poultry. One of its owners, Thomas Moss, purchased a horse and cart, which he kept out front to make deliveries. Moss's grocery cut into the business of a white grocer named William Barrett, who owned a store a few blocks away. Barrett began harassing Moss and trying to cause trouble at his store, resulting in several violent skirmishes between the two men and their employees. Late in March, six white men entered the People's Grocery carrying guns. Moss's men defended themselves, shooting and wounding three of their attackers. Afterward, Moss and two of his employees, Will Stewart and Calvin McDowell, were arrested and put into the Memphis city jail.

After they were arrested, Robert Church and the rest of the Tennessee Rifles kept watch over the jail to protect the men from being lynched. A few days later, the Rifles were given assurances that Moss and his men would not be charged and the police would protect them from lynching. Taking the authorities at their word, Church and the rest of the Rifles left. At 2 a.m., a lynch mob arrived at the jail. They entered and took Moss and his two men from their cell. The lynch mob had given the white papers notice of the lynching, and journalists met them at the rail yard where the execution was to be staged.

At the rail yard McDowell fought back against his lynchers. In retaliation, they shot and mutilated him before he was killed by multiple gunshots to the face. Will Stewart was next to die. He was stoic and strong and refused to show the lynchers any fear. The papers described him as "obdurate and unyielding to the last." He was shot on the right side of the neck with a shotgun, with a pistol in the neck and left eye, and then fell dead. Moss was the last to die. He begged for his life. When it was clear he would receive no mercy, he gave a final statement to the reporters present. "Tell my people to go West, there is no justice for them here," he said. His killers then shot him dead.

The lynching sent shock waves through the African American community. Church, who had believed that the law would protect the men after he left them, privately began to doubt the viability of the region as a home for African Americans. After the lynching, more than a hundred blacks formed a group to leave Tennessee and relocate to Oklahoma. Church donated $10,000 ($270,000) to the group. He would never leave. He'd been shackled, shot, and burned out, but for better or worse, Memphis was his home.

10

Building the Promised Land in Oklahoma

1893

Moments before noon on a hot and dusty day in September 1893, more than one hundred thousand men, women, and children lined up along the northern border of the Oklahoma territory like racers at the start line. They were "boomers," property seekers who had journeyed from across the country to the West in order to participate in what was shaping up to be the country's largest land run. More than a year earlier, the federal government had purchased 6,361,000 acres from the Cherokee tribe in the former Indian territory of Oklahoma and promised to open the land up for settlement to homesteaders on a first-arrive basis at exactly noon on September 16, 1893.

They began arriving almost a year before the run was to begin, in wagons and on the backs of horses and donkeys, camping along the Kansas-Oklahoma border. The camps were crowded, as farmers were facing hard times due to drought, declining profits in the agricultural sector, and an economic depression in 1893 (later known as the Panic of 1893). The overriding mood in the camps was one of desperation. Tens of thousands of boomers lived in tents and makeshift houses. Those who came early in the year endured Oklahoma's brief but frigid winter, followed by thunderstorms and tornado-like winds in the spring, and a hot and humid summer. Death seemed to linger in the air, due to outbreak of disease and food and water shortages. Gunfights and brawls between boomers were regular occurrences.

Among the frontiersmen was a twenty-five-year-old African American man named Ottowa W. Gurley. Gurley was well built, with a square jaw and broad shoulders. He had mahogany skin, angular features, and curly dark hair that he parted at the side. Like the other boomers, Gurley dreamed of a better life. He was the son of slaves, born on Christmas Day in 1868 in Huntsville, Alabama, to John and Rosanna Gurley. He grew up in Pine Bluff, Arkansas, on a farm with his family and attended public grammar school. Afterward he became a teacher and then later an employee of the United States Postal Service. He was ambitious yet pragmatic, and the government's public land handout in Oklahoma seemed like just the type of opportunity he'd be remiss to pass up.

At noon sharp on September 16, a cannon fired, marking the start of the run. The boom of the gun set off a stampede into the territory, as boomers sprinted across the Oklahoma border onto the state's green prairies and red sandy soil, kicking up clouds of dust. The boomers carried with them posts with their surnames written on them. When they found an available plot of land, they could lay their claim to it by driving the stake into the ground.

When they entered the Cherokee outpost, many found that most of the better land had already been taken by outlaws called "Sooners" who had sneaked into the territory early and squatted on the best areas. Nonetheless, thousands of boomers, black and white, planted their flags in the land that day and applied for their land permits.

Gurley traveled south for more than fifty miles through a forest of scrubby oak trees to a large prairie filled with thousands of tents of other boomers. There, Gurley staked his claim to a plot of dirt. Five days later, the area was incorporated as the town of Perry, Oklahoma, and Gurley was given the rights to the plot where he planted his flag.

AFRICAN AMERICANS HAD BEGUN TO RELOCATE TO THE FORMER Indian territory in Oklahoma as soon as it was open for settlement in 1889. The Central Oklahoma Emigration Society, an organization funded by Robert Reed Church, helped thousands of African Americans emigrate to Oklahoma to escape oppression, lynching, and terror in Memphis. These individuals were joined by groups of black homesteaders from Arkansas, Kentucky, Virginia, Washington, D.C., New York, the Carolinas, Georgia, and Florida, all seeking greater freedom and opportunity in an America where African Americans were beginning to face violent backlash for the gains they had made during Reconstruction.

They were led in establishing themselves in Oklahoma by Edward P. McCabe, an enterprising African American from Troy, New York. McCabe was thin, with straight hair, skin the color of sand, and a handlebar mustache. He wore three-piece suits, spectacles, and bow ties. Before the land runs, he had lobbied the US government in Washington, D.C., to make Oklahoma an all-black state. When his requests to establish a black Oklahoma were denied, he moved to the territory during the land runs in 1889 and began establishing a movement to build all-black towns in the state. Twenty-five miles south of the town of Perry, he built an all-black town and called his land of promise Langston. He was not alone in organizing a black town; between 1890 and 1900, black boomers in Oklahoma established more than thirty such towns. "McCabe proposes to establish at Langston a distinctly Negro city and has for months, through colonization societies, been working in the Southern states to secure a population for this new black Mecca," a *New*

York Times article stated in 1891. "There are nearly 200 persons already there, and not a white face is to be found in the place."

McCabe hired a half-dozen traveling salesmen and took out newspaper ads to promote black emigration to Oklahoma. Within a year, McCabe's town boasted more than two hundred residents. For McCabe, Langston was the beginning of a black takeover of Oklahoma. He believed that if he could get enough blacks to resettle in Oklahoma, black towns could join together to take over the state and make it an all-black region. By 1892, Langston had twenty-five businesses, a doctor, and a school. By 1895, the residents had telephone service. In 1897, a black college was established there.

MCCABE'S REPRESENTATIVES CRISSCROSSED THE COUNTRY RE-cruiting, appearing in black churches and meeting halls, boasting about the all-black towns where African Americans ruled. McCabe coordinated with the founders of other black towns in Oklahoma and in back rooms plotted together with them to one day take over the state. African Americans from Georgia, Mississippi, Alabama, and Florida began to migrate to the towns in small numbers as lynchings and violence increased and some became tired of the hard life and low wages of sharecropping. In the Oklahoma towns, blacks had their own institutions and community, and it seemed as though at last they had found a life free from oppression and terror.

Gurley moved his wife, Emma, to Perry with him from Arkansas. After getting settled, he attempted to find work. He ran for county treasurer but was defeated, and instead took a job as principal of the school in the new town as conciliation. Perry was a frontier town located on a mile-long prairie. In Perry's early days, its residents lived in and ran businesses out of tents and wood shacks. They supported themselves by operating cattle ranches and wheat farms, and they erected more than one hundred bars, restaurants, and shops in a business district in the center of the town. Gurley, seeing the wave of development in Perry, opened a general store, which was successful but did nothing to set Gurley apart from the other shop owners in town.

Perry was a multiracial place, with a large number of African Americans having settled there alongside white boomers and immigrants from Germany, Bohemia, and Russia. Edward P. McCabe attempted to establish an all-black town called Liberty near Perry in 1893, but the town failed to attract residents and proved to be short-lived.

MCCABE WAS STRUGGLING TO KEEP HIS DREAM OF A BLACK MECCA in Oklahoma alive. In the spring of 1896, the Supreme Court ruled in the case of *Plessy v. Ferguson.* The case, brought by a multiracial group of activists from New Orleans, brought a constitutional challenge to a set of laws passed by the Louisiana state legislature in 1890 that mandated separate but equal seating areas for blacks and whites on trains and buses. The Supreme Court, in a 7–1 decision, ruled to uphold the law and by extension confirm the right of states to pass racial-segregation laws. The ruling was the unofficial inauguration of the Jim Crow era, striking a final blow to the racially progressive epoch of Reconstruction.

In Oklahoma, white southerners moved into the territory and began to take over its government after the land run. They were led by William "Alfalfa Bill" Murray, a white segregationist and lawyer from Texas. Murray resembled a vaudeville villain, with tanned skin, yellow tobacco-stained teeth, and a drooping mustache. He moved to Oklahoma in 1899 and intermarried with the ruling family of the Chickasaw tribe. Bill shared the Chickasaws' hatred of blacks and opposed McCabe at every turn. "As a rule they are failures as lawyers," he once said in a thinly veiled barb, adding, "It is an entirely false notion that the Negro can rise to the equal of a white man in the professions or become an equal citizen." As he watched blacks build a town on the old Indian land, he lamented, "I appreciate the old time ex-slave, the old darky—and they are the salt of their race—who comes to me talking softly in that humble spirit which should characterize their actions and dealing with white men." Under his leadership, segregationists began to pass racist laws and restrict the voting rights of African Americans with grandfather and great-grandfather clauses. McCabe sold his house to create a war chest to fight the racist laws in court. However, he lost repeatedly in court fighting Alfalfa Bill and his band of white supremacists and went broke from the legal expenses. In the end, he was forced to leave the state after running out of money. In his absence, the segregationists gained even more power in Oklahoma and Alfalfa Bill was elected to the state legislature.* The region's small black towns followed McCabe's decline; many shuttered and emptied out. The promised land, for the moment, was lost.

* Bill "Alfalfa" Murray later became governor of Oklahoma in 1931. His son Johnston Murray also served as governor, in 1955.

11

Founding the Black Hair Industry

~~

On a cold evening in 1878, as snow fell, the winter winds swirled outside a small wood-frame house in Peoria, Illinois. Inside the kitchen with a black wood-burning stove at its center, Annie Minerva Turnbo stood on a wood crate behind her older sister Sarah, parting and plaiting Sarah's hair. Annie was nine years old with a round face the color of mahogany. She was small for her age and looked even tinier, draped in three sweaters and a thick pair of trousers to protect against the cold. She had an outsize personality and was quick-witted and precocious. As her small fingers wove through her sister's thick, curly hair, two of her sister's friends, Lilly and Bea, sat a few feet away at the kitchen table, making small talk and watching Annie. "She's got the knack,"

Lilly said. "She can do hair like nobody's business." "And it's going to be my business," said Annie as she continued to wrap sections of her sister's hair around her fingers and then weave them together. "You might have the knack, but that doesn't mean anything," Lilly cautioned Annie. "My granny makes the best fried catfish this side of the Ohio River, but that doesn't put food on the table or clothes on her back." Sarah chimed in as Annie moved on to another section of hair, "She might be able to charge a penny. She might even earn a little spending money on the side, when she gets a real job."

Annie's future seemed to come up any time the girls got together to have her work on their hair. Annie imagined that she would start a business doing hair and make enough money that she didn't have to work as a maid or on a farm as her sister and friends did. That type of thinking was what worried Sarah and her friends—"Annie's dream," they called it dismissively. In Peoria it was hard enough for African Americans, most of whom worked long hours as domestics in the mansions of the rich on the Illinois River waterfront, or as hands on the pig and cow ranches on the outskirts of town. In Peoria and many communities like it, Emancipation had left African Americans only a half step out of slavery. It seemed that the only jobs available for blacks were frustratingly similar to the ones they had worked before the Civil War. After Emancipation it was common for African Americans to be forced to work for the same families that had once enslaved them. Sarah and her friends warned Annie not to put her hopes in foolish dreams. Who had ever heard of a black hair business, anyway?

Annie and Sarah had endured enough suffering already. Sarah, Annie's parents, and Annie's other older siblings had been enslaved in Kentucky, on a plantation near the childhood home of Abraham Lincoln. When the Civil War began, her father, Robert Turnbo, had enlisted in the Fifth Kentucky Cavalry of the Union Army and sent his wife, Isabel, and his children on the Underground Railroad to the free soil of Illinois. In 1866, he surrendered his horse and gun, hung up his blue Union uniform and cap, and trekked to Illinois to reunite with his family, hoping they could build a better life in the emancipated world. One of his first acts as a free man was to go to city hall and apply for a marriage license. He bought a farm in Metropolis, Illinois, where he and his family worked the soil for their own gain, not that of a plantation owner.

On August 9, 1869, the Turnbos welcomed their tenth child, a girl whom they named Annie Minerva Turnbo. In the years after slavery, black farmers like the Turnbos faced a world that was both free and perilous. Black farmers, if they could bring in a good crop, could make as much as or more than white farmers. However, in addition to the backbreaking labor of farming, they also faced threats of violence from white supremacist groups. In some cases, the groups would damage their crops, kill their livestock, or threaten their very lives. When Annie was a toddler, Isabel and Robert Turnbo fell ill, and died within months of each other, leaving

Annie an orphan. She then went to live with her adult sister Laura in the nearby town of Peoria. She slept on a cot in the kitchen of her sister's small house, the same room where she worked on Sarah and her friends' hair in her spare time.

"She'd sure earn a penny if she could fix that hair of yours," Lilly cracked, motioning toward Bea, the other friend, who had been sitting silently at the table. Bea had a blue scarf tied around her head, covering her hair. She had dark brown skin and big brown eyes, which she cast downward, frowning in response to Lilly's remark. "It's your own fault," Lilly admonished her. Bea had been using a hair straightener she had purchased from a traveling salesman that had caused her hair to fall out. "You might as well jump in a river of lye as to put that mess in your hair," Lilly said. "Can you help?" Bea asked, looking at Annie. She lifted the scarf to reveal that half of her head was hairless. Annie got down from the crate she was standing on and walked over to the table to take a closer look. The skin on Bea's head was red and swollen. "I thought you learned your lesson," Sarah said to Bea unsympathetically. Bea seemed to be obsessed with changing her appearance. She had tried skin-lightening tablets, which contained cyanide, skin-bleaching creams, and whitening powders. Recently, she had bought a whitening lotion, which had irritated the skin on her arms and hands.

The black beauty industry in the years after slavery ended was dominated by traveling salesmen and beauty companies that sold products to alter the appearance of African Americans to make them look more like white people. Black skin removers, whitening pills, and hair straighteners were advertised in pamphlets, broadsides, and flyers with the goal of ostensibly helping black people to assimilate into white society. The products were snake oil but sold well, in part because some black people believed that looking whiter would help them achieve higher self-esteem and social status. Lye soaps and tins of animal fat were the most common hair products used by African Americans in those years. Hair was more of a social institution than a business; women had their hair braided and styled by family members or friends in their homes, usually with no money being exchanged. At the time, it was hard to imagine anyone making it into a business.

During enslavement, African Americans had been treated as chattel and been deprived of adequate clothing and soap. As a result, there was no defined black aesthetic or hair care in the years after Emancipation. Black women often wore braided styles adapted from African hair-braiding techniques. Or, like Mary Ellen Pleasant, they kept their hair hidden under bonnets and scarves. Black men, such as Frederick Douglass and Robert Reed Church, cut their own hair, then slicked it back with bear oil, imitating the hairstyles of white men as best they could. The New York millionaire Jeremiah Hamilton chose to shave his head of tightly coiled hair, which the newspapers referred to as "wool," and wear a wig of straight black hair. In 1878, as Annie dreamed of having a hair business, black beauty was yet to be defined or commodified.

White beauty salons and barbershops, on the other hand, were booming and were often run by black men and women. Robert Reed Church's first wife, Louisa, made a small fortune dressing white women's hair and wigs in Memphis. She used her money to help her husband open his first business and buy the family's first home and a horse-drawn carriage. In Atlanta, Alonzo Herndon, a former slave, opened the "Crystal Palace," the most famous barbershop for white men in the South, the beginning of a million-dollar business empire. It would be years before the Herndons and the Churches would become well known as the richest black families in the South, so to Sarah and her friends, Annie's insistence that she could turn black hair into a business was more foolish than visionary.

"Maybe your hair will be better when it grows out," Annie said as she finished examining Bea's head. "If it grows out!" Lilly jabbed. Bea put her head into her hands, shook it from side to side, and began to cry. "All I wanted," she said, her voice breaking and cracking, "was to look nice—you know, pretty."

Bea's problem wasn't uncommon. With their scalps damaged by chemicals and their hair follicles clogged by heavy oils, many women like Bea were losing their hair. Annie might have been good at styling hair, but getting it to grow again was another matter.

⤳

ABOUT A WEEK LATER, IN THE MIDDLE OF THE NIGHT, ANNIE awoke in a coughing fit. She flailed about, gasping for air and tugging at the neck of her nightgown. Sarah was awakened by the noise and rushed into the kitchen. She put a pot of water on the stove, lit a fire, and threw a handful of herbs from a jar into the water. Then she opened the front door and let a rush of cold into the kitchen. When the chilly air hit Annie in the face, she gasped. Her airways opened slightly. Sarah snatched her up and held her face over the pot of boiling water, telling her to inhale the steam coming off the herbs in the boiling pot. After an hour, she was breathing normally and Sarah put her to bed.

Annie stayed in bed for three days after the incident. On the fourth day, she asked to return to school. "You're not going anywhere, you're at death's door," Sarah told her. Sarah kept Annie in the house until spring. One warm day in April, she sent her out on an errand to buy some herbs from the local herbalist. She handed Annie a jar made of clay with money in it. "Don't dawdle," she told her, pressing it into her chest. Annie took the pot and headed out, leaving the house for the first time in months.

The herbalist lived in a cabin in the woods just outside the city. Annie wandered to the outskirts of Peoria until she reached a dirt path. She followed the path through an open field, past a grove of walnut trees, past a creek, and up and down a hill, to where the herbalist lived in a cottage by a small creek-fed pond. There she saw a woman working in the garden in the front yard of the house. She wore an apron with dozens of pockets, which she was stuffing with flowers and leaves that she picked from the garden. Annie went up to her and handed her the clay pot.

The woman greeted Annie. "You still having those spells, Annie?" Annie nodded. "You'll grow out of those spells," the woman told her and then led her inside the house. The aromatic house was filled with shelves of labeled jars containing herbs and oils. The woman pulled three jars from the shelf and led Annie to a table, where she sprinkled some of the herbs from each jar into a mortar and crushed them together with a pestle. As the woman worked, Annie wandered the room looking at the jars on the wall; "Sage, cures coughs," "Feverfew, cures rheumatism," and "Valerian root, brings sleep." As she read the labels on the hundreds of jars, they seemed to offer a cure for any ailment thinkable—heartbreak, weight gain, teeth grinding. Suddenly, Annie remembered Bea and her hair loss problem.

"Do you have anything for hair?" she asked. "A plant that grows hair?"

"No," the herbalist said, "I have many."

She took down three jars of herbs, sprinkled some of each into her mortar, and crushed them. She then took down a thick, creamy yellow liquid and mixed

Annie Malone, 1922 *(St. Louis Post-Dispatch)*

Hannah Elias, 1903 *(New York Public Library, Astor, Lenox and Tilden Foundations, Evening World)*

John Mott Drew with sons and bus *(Wills family)*

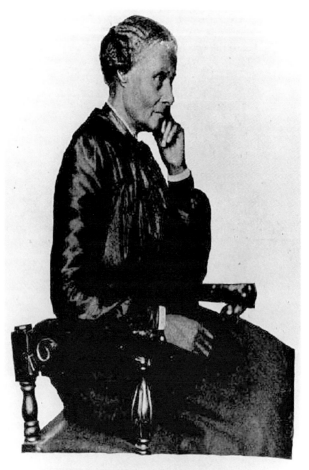

MARY ELLEN ("MAMMY") PLEASANT AT 87 YEARS OF AGE
The first and only photograph taken since she was 13 years old

Mary Ellen Pleasant, 1901 *(Bancroft Library)*

Robert Reed Church, 1899 *(University of Tennessee)*

President Theodore Roosevelt speaking at
Robert Reed Church's park, 1902 *(University of Tennessee)*

Church Auditorium, built by Robert Reed Church, 1904 (*University of Tennessee*)

The mansion Mary Ellen Pleasant built for her business partner, Thomas Bell, 1908 (*Bancroft Library*)

some of it into the herbs. "This is a hair elixir," she told Annie. "Just take some of it and rub it into your scalp and let it sit for thirty minutes." She pushed the mixture toward Annie. "Now that'll be a dime," she added. Annie took the mixture along with the herbs her sister had asked her to buy and headed home.

The next time Bea came over, Annie told her about the concoction and asked if she could try it on her. Bea agreed, and Annie applied the substance to her scalp. After a few days, Bea's skin started to heal. A few weeks after that, her hair started to grow back. Annie's health continued to improve that spring, but Sarah kept her out of school, fearing that she was too weak. Annie asked Bea to get her science books to study while she was out of school. Bea was grateful to Annie for curing her baldness and got her mother, who worked as a cleaning woman at the white school in Peoria, to borrow books from the school, which she gave to Annie.

Throughout her childhood, Annie read anything about chemistry, biology, and hygiene she could get her hands on, hoping she could learn something about hair. One day she came across a text on dairy farmers' use of ointments to treat the skin of cows' udders. After reading about the ointments, she went into town, purchased a cow ointment from the drugstore, took it home, and mixed in various hair-growing herbs from the herbalist. She tried the ointment on a stray cat she found suffering from mange. The solution seemed to help regrow some of the animal's hair after a few applications. She decided it was time to try it on a person.

She tried out her concoction on one of Sarah's friends who had tried to straighten her hair with lye soap and burned her scalp. She had bald patches all over her head where she had scalded herself with the straightening substance. When the friend came to Annie, she washed her head, then applied her new solution of ointment and herbs. After she was done, the friend asked her how long it would take for her hair to start growing again. "I don't know," Annie replied. "You are my first human experiment." The friend returned a few days later to show Annie that the patches that had been bald were now sprouting hair. The solution had worked. Annie had invented her own hair elixir.

Next Annie began to make her own elixir by copying the ingredients used in cow ointment: petroleum, sulfur, and lanolin or beeswax. Over the next ten years, she continued to treat women in Peoria, using them as test subjects to perfect her solution, tweaking its ingredients and their proportions. The sulfur removed damaged tissue, and the petroleum and beeswax helped heal chemical burns and moisten the skin. She added herbs she learned about from the herbalist that were purported to grow hair faster. She named her invention the Wonderful Hair Grower.

Annie's reputation grew in Peoria, as not only could she do hair "like nobody's business" but she could help women who were going bald from the chemicals sold by traveling salesmen grow hair again. It was a small miracle.

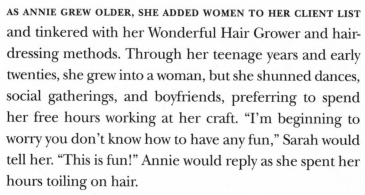

AS ANNIE GREW OLDER, SHE ADDED WOMEN TO HER CLIENT LIST and tinkered with her Wonderful Hair Grower and hair-dressing methods. Through her teenage years and early twenties, she grew into a woman, but she shunned dances, social gatherings, and boyfriends, preferring to spend her free hours working at her craft. "I'm beginning to worry you don't know how to have any fun," Sarah would tell her. "This is fun!" Annie would reply as she spent her hours toiling on hair.

By Annie's thirtieth birthday, in 1899, she had more than two hundred clients, the majority of the three hundred or so black women in town, but she still wasn't making much money. She had dropped out of school and had to work odd jobs to help Sarah with the household bills. Annie was unmarried, overworked, and barely getting by, but she was undeterred. She decided what she needed was a larger customer base.

At the turn of the century, Annie and Sarah moved to Lovejoy, Illinois, to try to turn the Wonderful Hair Grower into a full-time business. Lovejoy, now called Brooklyn, was the oldest incorporated black town in the United States. The city had been founded by escaped and emancipated slaves from St. Louis in the early 1830s. Its black population was twice the size of Peoria's. With any luck, Annie could double her business.

Annie and Sarah rented an office for $5 ($146) a month in the back of a wood building near the town's main street. The day they moved in, Annie took out a piece of paper and scribbled down the rent, then wrote an amount for supplies and living expenses under it. She added up the numbers and showed the total to Sarah. "That's how much we have to make if we want to be here a second month."

Annie then left the office and went for a stroll around town. She noted the location of the drugstore, where they could purchase their supplies. She kept walking, stopping to note the locations of the black churches and the houses where women's clothes were drying on the laundry lines. Those are where our potential customers are, she thought. She hurried back to the office and drew a map from memory of where she thought they could find customers.

The next day, just after sunrise, she set out. She had divided the map she was carrying into six sections. She would canvass one section of the map per day. She went from door to door and told women about her hair products. By the end of the week, she had covered the entire town. However, her initial solicitations weren't fruitful. Most of the women thought she was another snake oil merchant and were dubious of her claim that she could regrow hair.

Annie decided she needed to do something dramatic to convince the women of her new town that her product worked. She dug into her and Sarah's savings and rented a horse and buggy. She loaded the buggy with her products, buckets of hot water, and a chair.

She went around the town searching for a gathering of women leaving church or running errands. She would stop the buggy and lecture the women on the importance of proper hygiene and hair care. Afterward she'd do one of the women's hair on the cart free of charge. Her demonstrations won over women at nearly every stop. At the end of the month, Annie and Sarah had earned more than enough to stay another month.

After Annie had been in Lovejoy for a few months, a teenage girl named Alice visited Annie in her office. By then Annie's business was thriving, and Alice had heard that Annie could work miracles with hair. She carried with her a picture she had torn from a magazine and handed it to Annie. "Can you make my hair look like this?" she asked. The picture was of a "Gibson Girl." The woman in the picture was white with pale skin, ruddy cheeks, and straight hair pinned in waves on top of her head. Annie was puzzled; how could a black woman be made to look like a Gibson Girl? She led the girl to her salon chair. "You're too beautiful to try to look like something you're not," she told her. "I'm going to give you my Wonderful Hair Grower treatment." "Just like the Gibson Girl?" Alice asked excitedly. "I can't do that and wouldn't if I could," Annie responded. "But I won't do anything until you stop talking about the Gibson Girl, agreed?" Annie said warmly. "But I'm tired of it in my eyes," Alice explained. She was in stenography school, and her hair, which dropped over her forehead, dripped sweat into her eyes. Annie washed and combed Alice's curly hair and pinned it behind her head. She then took the strands on Alice's forehead and neck and pinned them to her head with a set of ornamented combs. After she finished, she handed Alice a mirror. "I'd like to say you look like the ideal American beauty," she told her. Alice was smiling as she looked herself over. Annie paused and thought a moment. "Would you like a job selling the Wonderful Hair Grower?" she asked. Alice was overjoyed and wanted to start that afternoon. It had taken Annie several weeks to win over the women of Lovejoy; perhaps hiring a local who could give firsthand testimony of the benefits of her products would make selling more efficient. Soon after hiring Alice, Annie hired two more Lovejoy women as salespeople.

A few weeks after she was hired, Alice came into Annie's office and laid another piece of paper before her. "Is this another Gibson Girl?" Annie asked with exasperation. Alice laughed. "Here's your chance," she said, turning the paper over.

THE LOUISIANA PURCHASE EXPOSITION

Meet the World in St. Louis in 1903
People from around the country.
Representatives from around the world
will be in St. Louis in 1903 at
The World's Fair

IN 1903, ANNIE MOVED TO ST. LOUIS TO TRY TO CAPITALIZE ON the excitement and population growth occurring in the city in anticipation of the World's Fair. In the years leading up to the fair, more than twelve thousand people moved to St. Louis to take jobs working in the construction crews building the fairgrounds in the city park. Annie rented an apartment in downtown St. Louis with indoor plumbing, a kitchen and bathroom, a bedroom, and a separate living room. The streets of downtown St. Louis were filled with horse-drawn buggies and streetcars. Telephone poles lined the busy sidewalk where men, women, and children moved among office buildings made of brick and brownstone, hotels, theaters, and shops.

In her first few nights in St. Louis Annie couldn't sleep. The sound of fire engines blaring and street traffic seemed extremely loud compared to the country towns in Illinois where she had spent all of her thirty-four years. She wondered how she could accomplish anything in St. Louis without a good night's sleep, but after a few days she got used to the noise and slept soundly.

She set out on the town with a case of product samples and began knocking on doors. She had a full line of products to go along with her Wonderful Hair Grower: cleansing cream, shampoo, face powder, and assorted cosmetics. On one of her outings, she happened upon a small apartment building in the colored section of town. She knocked on the door and was greeted by a woman named Sarah Breedlove. Breedlove had a stocky build, brown skin, a round face with wide-set eyes, and a broad nose. One of the first things Annie noticed was her hair. It was short and matted, and her scalp was dry and flaky and had bald spots. She convinced Breedlove to let her come in and shampoo her hair. She was wearing expensive clothes and her hair was, as it always was, clean and pinned behind her head.

As Annie shampooed her hair, Breedlove told Annie that she was a widow and mother and had immigrated to St. Louis from Louisiana. She lived with her seventeen-year-old daughter, A'Lelia, and worked as a laundress in St. Louis. Like Annie, she was the daughter of enslaved African Americans and had become an orphan when her parents had died when she was a girl. The two women connected as Annie washed and detangled her curly hair, massaged her scalp, and applied her Wonderful Hair Grower to the skin on her head, which was covered with dandruff and scabs. Annie then told Breedlove about herself. She offered Breedlove a job selling her products and promised that not only would her hair grow back, but she would make more money than she did as a laundress. Breedlove accepted Annie's offer and within a few weeks was one of her best saleswomen in the region.

THE WORLD'S FAIR BEGAN ON APRIL 30, 1904, HAVING BEEN POST-poned a year due to its growing in scope and size. The event was staged on a 1,272-acre park in the middle of the city. President Theodore Roosevelt attended the fair along with more than two hundred thousand Missourians and tourists from all over the country and the world. There were nine hundred buildings made of white stone, statues, man-made lakes, a zoo, and villages where Apache Indians, Congolese Pygmies, and Filipinos lived in huts and tepees and wore tribal garb. The grounds, which were interconnected by looping dirt roads, curved through the grass. There was also a train, which visitors could ride for ten cents.

Annie, at thirty-four years of age, had never left the Midwest. The World's Fair, however, brought the world to her. At the fair Annie met black tourists from the South, the West, the East, and the Caribbean and pitched their selling her products in their hometowns. She used the opportunity to begin building a national sales network and take her company from a regional business to a global brand.

Annie visited the fair as often as she could for the year it ran. She was particularly fascinated with the exhibit of Africans at the fair called "African Wilds." The exhibit spanned more than 40 acres of the park. There, hundreds of African men, women, and children lived in huts made of sticks and leaves and dressed in loincloths. Around this time, she named her company Poro Products. She chose the name, in part, because it sounded like an African word, and Annie was fascinated with the continent of the tribesmen at the fair and her ancestors.

Shortly after the World's Fair, Sarah Breedlove met with Annie to tell her she was moving to Denver, Colorado. Her hair had grown back in and was full and thick. She offered to sell Annie's product in Colorado. Annie agreed that it was a good idea and wished her well in her travels. She did not have a sales rep in Colorado, whose black population was growing rapidly as so-called Exodusters, black refugees from the Jim Crow South, were settling there by the hundreds.

Breedlove took the train to Denver with her daughter, her belongings, and a supply of Poro products to sell. She sold Poro products in her new city and worked part-time as a laundress. A few months into her move, her boyfriend from St. Louis, a traveling salesman named Charles James "C. J." Walker, moved to Denver. They married a few months later. Charles convinced his new wife that she should stop selling Annie's products and they should start their own line. Annie hadn't trademarked the name or the formulas and was powerless to stop the copycatting.

12

Black Cleopatra

Winter 1884
PHILADELPHIA, PENNSYLVANIA

On a wintry evening in 1883, couriers, mounted on horses and dressed in top hats and coats, cantered through the streets of Philadelphia's Seventh Ward. They cut through winds that tore at their faces and rattled the branches of trees lining the streets as they went from house to house knocking on doors. When the residents answered, the messengers placed an envelope in their hands.

The Seventh Ward of Philadelphia, one of America's first free black neighborhoods, had been founded by freed slaves in the eighteenth century and now contained more than six thousand black residents, many of them recent immigrants from former slave territories. The area, colloquially known as the "colored colony," was a framework of residential streets that stretched from the city center to the mouth of the Schuylkill River. Until the late hours of the evening, its porches and sidewalks were filled with black men, women, and children, socializing or coming to or from work or errands.

The envelopes that were delivered protected a smaller envelope within them, which when opened revealed a card with crisp lettering. The card announced the wedding of Hattie, the eldest daughter of Charles Elias, the upcoming spring at the First Union Baptist Church.

The men and women of the settlement were both surprised and excited to receive the invitations, as weddings were not a common event. More than half of the four thousand adults in the settlement were in common-law marriages, cohabited with lovers, or were lifelong bachelors and bachelorettes. Such arrangements were a remnant of plantation life, where enslaved people rarely married, as they needed the consent of their owners to do so legally.

The colony was buzzing in anticipation as the day of Hattie Elias's wedding approached. "It was to be one of the most remembered events in the colored colony," one invitee remembered.

The Eliases were a family of eleven headed by Charles Elias, a caterer, and his wife, Mary. They lived in a three-story town house on a street inhabited by the settlement's wealthiest black residents: doctors, dentists, preachers, lawyers, and undertakers. Neighbors considered them "fairly well-to-do" but not wealthy.

As a caterer, Elias was respected as an artisan in one of black America's oldest trades. Beginning in the late eighteenth century, freed people who had worked as cooks on plantations took up catering. It became one of the first businesses in America whose proprietors included a substantial number of blacks. As a result, caterers, even years after slavery ended, enjoyed a special, almost honorific status within black communities.

Elias labored to move his family to a wealthy block and place himself among the top caterers in the colony. Hattie's wedding, with any luck, would mark the ascension of the Eliases as one of the leading Negro families in the colony.

As the wedding approached, Elias planned an impressive menu for the reception that would follow the nuptials: a spread of pickled vegetables and eggs, soup, fowl, and baked ham would be served, followed by a wedding cake—a confection of flour, butter, sugar, molasses, and fruit covered in white icing. It was to be a Baptist wedding, so there would be no drinking or dancing, making the food second in importance only to the bride herself.

There was no concern in that regard. Like all the Elias daughters, Hattie had both appealing looks and evident refinement. The Elias children were slender with a sandy-colored complexion like their mother's. They had also inherited what many considered their father's best trait: almond-shaped brown eyes, that he liked to attribute to having "Indian blood in 'em." The children all attended colored public schools, and in addition to learning reading and arithmetic, they studied painting and music.

If there was an exception to the fine breeding of the Elias children, it was the youngest daughter of the family, eighteen-year-old Hannah Bessie, who was described by neighbors as "precocious." She had never been in any real trouble but had a reputation for seeking attention, which could have been attributed to her youth.

The streets were brimming with pink, purple, green, and red in the spring of 1885, as the shadbush, sugar plum, and hawthorn trees growing along the sidewalks of Philadelphia's streets began to bloom. On a warm evening, nearly a thousand guests filed into the chapel of First Union Baptist Church for Hattie Elias's wedding. It was one of the largest churches in the settlement, two stories with a stone exterior, pitched roof, and stained-glass windows trimmed with red stucco. Candles lit up the sanctuary as attendees filled the pews and balcony. Hattie wore a white dress of lace and satin, which her father had commissioned just for the occasion. The ceremony, an opening prayer and sermon followed by the exchange of vows, was short and occurred without incident. As guests made their way from the chapel to the fellowship hall, where Charles Elias was readying a banquet, their attention began to drift elsewhere.

All eyes rested on his youngest daughter, Hannah. She was wearing a ball gown that looked costly and elaborate. One guest described it as "a wonderful creation," while others gathered around her to get a better view. When the affair let out late that night, it was widely agreed that Hannah Elias had been "the belle of the evening."

Not much more was made of Hannah's dress until several days later, when a group of police officers arrived unexpectedly at the Elias house looking for Hannah. They held in their hands a warrant for her arrest for larceny from her employer. Hannah worked in the home of a wealthy white woman in North Philadelphia who had heard about the dress that Hannah had worn to Hattie's wedding and concluded that Hannah had borrowed a dress from her without consent. The officers arrested her on the spot and took her to the Button Street police station, where they placed her in a holding cell to await trial. That evening she went before the judge and was convicted of larceny and sentenced to four months in Moyamensing Prison in South Philadelphia.

A HORSE-DRAWN WAGON ARRIVED AT THE POLICE STATION TO transport Hannah Elias to Moyamensing Prison. An officer placed her in the back of the covered wagon, as the coachman settled into the driver's seat and grabbed the horse's reins. As the carriage galloped along dirt and cobblestone streets, Elias sat in the dark contemplating what awaited her.

When they came to a stop, she was removed from the wagon and taken into a compound bounded by a stone wall. In front of her she saw a building made of white stone with a guard tower rising from its center and barred windows looking out onto the fenced grounds. She had arrived at Moyamensing Prison.

Moyamensing was designed to resemble the tomb of an Egyptian pharaoh. Its exterior was made of limestone with walls slanted in like those of a pyramid. Around its entrances were columns and hieroglyphic carvings. The architects of the structure had envisioned prisoners being overcome with the sensation that they were going to their deaths when they entered it. Elias was taken to the main entrance of the building and through a set of tall wooden doors. The entryway opened up into a cell block containing rows of rooms holding men behind iron bars.

The prison was spread over three floors and housed more than three hundred inmates, most of them men. The first floor, where Elias entered, held convicts guilty of murder and other violent crimes. The second and third floors housed nonviolent offenders. Elias was taken to a section of the second floor, where the prison's forty or so female inmates were housed.

Her days inside were lonely and unmarked by activities to help her pass the time. Prisoners were kept in solitary confinement and took all their meals in the cell where they slept. Guards paced the hallways of the cell blocks, chastising inmates for speaking across the hall to one another or making noise of any sort. The only events were a daily shoemaking class in a back room and a morning sermon given from the hallway. The chaplain often quoted from scriptures such as Acts 3:19: "Herefore, repent and turn to him to have your sins blotted out"; Ezekiel 18:30: "Repent! And turn from all your transgressions, so iniquity will not be your ruin"; and other similar scriptures about turning away from a life of sin.

After four months in Moyamensing, Hannah Elias was set free. Upon receiving her walking papers, she set out for her family's house in the Negro settlement. When she arrived, her father answered the door but blocked her entry. Charles, whom Hannah had not seen since she was arrested, was still worked up over the embarrassment of her arrest. He sent her away, banishing her from the family home indefinitely. For the next three months, she was not seen or heard from.

⌐⌐

IT WAS ALMOST SUNRISE AS JOHN R. PLATT AND HIS FRIENDS staggered through the streets of the Tenderloin district in Manhattan, bumping into men stumbling home drunk or dragging girls into alleys and hotels. On street corners and from the entrances to homes, prostitutes in tightly laced bustiers and bonnets topped with feathers propositioned them as they passed by.

The Tenderloin, a poor neighborhood of blacks and European immigrants, was the city's largest red-light district, stretching from 23rd to 42nd Streets in the heart of midtown Manhattan. It was controlled by organized crime families who bribed city officials to turn a blind eye to the brothels, peep shows, saloons, and gambling joints that operated out of the row houses that lined its streets.

That night, Platt and his group had been in the Tenderloin drinking and fornicating for hours and showed no signs of tiring. Given that the men were all in their sixties, it was an impressive show of stamina. They were, however, growing bored. Platt recalled that "having seen everything lively among the whites, someone said they wanted to see some coon joints."

Fulfilling that request fell to Platt, the group's guide for the evening. He was the owner of a glass-manufacturing company in New York and resided there with his wife and their children. His guests were retired firefighters from San Francisco visiting on holiday. Platt thought back to when he had visited them in San Francisco in 1864, remembering, "They showed me the time of my life in 'Frisco." It was late, but he felt obliged to press on and he knew just where they could find a black establishment.

Platt took his men to a "resort" that operated out of a house owned by an acquaintance, Julius "Pop" Miller, on the south side of the Tenderloin. A mulatto woman whose name he couldn't recall ran the operation. The men entered the house and stepped into a room decorated with carpet, a few pieces of furniture, and oil paintings on the wall and filled with teenage black girls. Platt's friends grabbed girls and retired to corners and back rooms. Platt ended up with Hannah Elias, who introduced herself as Bessie.

Platt was sixty-four years old, forty-five years Elias's senior. The contrast between them appeared even greater when they were near each other. Platt had lines under his eyes and pale skin, and both his beard and hair were turning white. Elias was nineteen but appeared to be just past puberty. Platt guessed that "she was a little girl of 15 or 16," when he first saw her.

She was thin and had a round face with a flat nose and big brown eyes with heavy eyelids. Her hair was dark and curly, and she kept it pinned back, with bangs draping down her forehead in front. She was confident and smart, which, along with her girlish appearance, charmed many male visitors. One of the girls who worked with Elias summed her up this way: "She exhibited a peculiar influence over white men."

Taken with his companion, Platt spent the rest of the evening at the house in her company. He would return several more times after their first encounter to see her until one night he went to call on her and was told she had left the house.

FRANK P. SATTERFIELD HAD BEEN COURTING ELIAS BEFORE SHE was jailed. He worked in a drugstore near Hannah's father's home in Philadelphia and had been calling on her frequently until her arrest. He was poor but well regarded, the neighbors describing him as "a bright young negro." Unfazed by the scandal, Satterfield planned to continue his pursuit of Hannah when she returned from prison. He went to the Elias residence after her release but was told that she had been banned from the house by her father and her whereabouts were unknown. The news seemed to increase his determination to be with her, and he enlisted the help of her twin brother, David, to search for her.

After three months, Satterfield and David found Hannah Elias living in a "resort" in New York's Tenderloin district. When David and Satterfield arrived, they pleaded with her to leave. She refused at first but later consented when Satterfield suggested that she move in with him in Philadelphia.

Satterfield lived in a room that he rented in an alleyway house on one of east Philadelphia's poorer streets. The house itself was falling apart. Elias found that unacceptable and began to badger the house's mistress to repair the place. After weeks of squabbling, the police were summoned to the house one night, when a fight broke out between the mistress and Elias. The boardinghouse's proprietor was arrested and jailed for thirty days as a result of the incident.

In March 1885, Elias became pregnant. The news left Satterfield distraught. He told her he could not support the child and urged her to apply for aid from the city. In the winter of 1885, Elias was given a place in the maternity ward of a Philadelphia almshouse. There, in early 1886, she delivered a baby girl whom she named Clara. While she was giving birth, Satterfield skipped town.

Abandoned and penniless, Elias decided to give the child up for adoption. After her daughter had been placed with another family, she began to search for Satterfield. She discovered that he was in New York, working as a clerk at a drugstore in Greenwich Village. In September 1887, she traveled to New York to confront him.

She showed up at the drugstore where he worked and was thrown out almost immediately by the owner of the store after she caused a scene. Undeterred, she waited outside for Satterfield for several hours and followed him home, screaming at him, while he refused to engage with her. When he arrived at his home, Satterfield summoned the police and had her arrested for harassment.

On September 18, 1887, Elias went before a judge at the Mercer Street police station in Manhattan to answer Satterfield's complaint against her. She told the judge that Satterfield had fathered a child with her and abandoned her. Satterfield did not show up in court that day but instead sent a sworn affidavit. The document stated that he had known Hannah Elias for ten years and that she was a "common woman." Taking Satterfield's implication that Elias was a prostitute into consideration, the judge found her guilty of disorderly conduct and sentenced her to a month in the prison on Blackwell's Island.

BLACKWELL'S ISLAND, NOW CALLED ROOSEVELT ISLAND, JUST OFF midtown Manhattan in the East River, contained three prisons and an asylum. The prisoners there spent their days breaking rocks or digging ditches outside with a ball and chain attached to their ankles. During breaks, they'd watch Manhattan millionaires sail by in yachts on the East River. At night, they jostled for bed space in the cell blocks, which held at least twice as many prisoners as intended. After thirty days, Elias left Blackwell's Island, on October 16, 1887, relieved to be gone.

She found lodging in East Midtown, a neighborhood of tenement homes, slaughterhouses, and factories populated by working-class blacks and European immigrants. Once she was situated, she decided to contact her former admirer, John R. Platt, from the Tenderloin.

Elias and Platt had once come up with a system to find each other if they lost track of each other. Using their pet names for each other—Bessie and Popper—one would post an ad in the paper inquiring where the other was. "Bessie, it's Popper, where are you?" it might say, to which the other would respond with a location: "Popper, it's Bessie, Dime Savings Bank 8:30."

When Platt laid eyes on Elias again in 1887, his eyes traced her curves and breasts, and he thought to himself that "the pretty little octoroon girl had now grown into full womanhood." Platt was married, but he would sneak away from his family as often as he could to rendezvous with her in the room she rented in a run-down tenement house near the East River.

Platt lived off of Fifth Avenue near the Vanderbilts and the Carnegies on "Millionaires' Row." He was the owner of a plate glass manufacturing company and had captured a number of the region's most lucrative accounts over the years, including the glass contract for the New York State Capitol in Albany and the Metropolitan Opera House in Manhattan. According to tax records, he took home an annual salary of just under a million dollars.

As Elias was getting reacquainted with her wealthy admirer, movements against the economic elite were sweeping the nation. In Washington, D.C., federal officials were vowing to crack down on big business by enacting "trust-busting" laws. Meanwhile, in industrial cities and mining towns, labor groups were organizing strikes and protests, and in New York anarchists were publishing essays maligning the wealthy and even beginning to plot assassination attempts on industrialists and aristocrats.

It was the beginning of what would later be called the Progressive Era of the 1890s, and it meant increased scrutiny of the lives and practices of the rich by the public, journalists, and the government. Men like Platt feared that any transgression, if revealed, could grow into a scandal.

Platt told Elias that their affair would have to remain secret, but, perhaps as a consolation, he offered to support her financially. After she agreed to carry on with him covertly, Platt began wiring her between $2,000 and $6,000 (between $58,000 and $175,000) every month.

He made sure she invested some of the money in bonds and real estate, reminding her that she needed to make the money last. "He said that he could not remember me in his will on account of his relatives," Elias recalled.

In 1890, Elias married Christopher Smith, a black railroad worker in his twenties. After her marriage, her arrangement with Platt went for the most part unchanged. Platt and Elias continued seeing each other whenever they could slip away from their spouses.

It seemed to be a workable arrangement for both of them until early in 1893, when Platt's wife died. A few months after her death, Elias recalled that Platt visited her, wanting to commit himself to her. As a token of the occasion, he presented Elias with a purse and watch that had belonged to his dead wife. Elias initially told him she couldn't accept them and suggested that he give them to his daughters. Platt was insistent; "he told me he loved me best of anyone in the world," she recalled him saying before she accepted his offering.

That year Platt helped Elias go into business as a boardinghouse operator. With his help, she purchased a house near his family residence where she could rent out rooms. The business would help her generate additional income and also provide Platt and Elias with a meeting place close to his home.

One night in 1895, when Platt showed up to visit her at the lodging house, one of her tenants, a man named Cornelius Williams, answered the door. Williams, twenty-six years old, had a thick build, thin mustache, dark complexion, and high forehead. He was preparing to go out for the evening when Platt rang the buzzer. "Are the folks in?" Platt asked as he stood on the house's porch in the dark. The question provoked anger in Williams for some reason, and he began to chide Platt.

"I didn't like his style," Williams remembered thinking. "I didn't want him around there." Williams slammed the door, only to open it a moment later to study the details of Platt's face. Then he slammed the door again. Still incensed, Williams asked one of the servants at the house about the man. She told him it was Mr. Green, an alias Platt used when visiting the house.

Elias evicted Williams a few weeks after the incident for reasons that remain unknown. He and Elias were members of the same church, Mount Olivet Baptist Church in Midtown, making for awkwardness as they passed each other in church on Sundays. Williams eventually left but did so swearing that Elias had bad-mouthed him to the congregation and turned it against him.

In 1897, Christopher Smith decided he had enough of Elias and Platt's affair and sued Platt for "alienating the affections of his wife." Platt gave Smith $500 ($6,863) to settle the suit and helped Elias file for a divorce. During the course of the proceedings, a lawyer whom Elias hired, August C. Nanz, demanded "legal fees" of $20,000 ($274,520) to keep Platt and Elias's affair secret. Platt paid the "fee," and Elias's divorce from Smith was finalized that year.

IN 1899, ELIAS MOVED OUT OF HER MARITAL HOME AND INTO A mansion on Central Park West purchased for her by Platt. Her new residence was part of a collection of homes along the park meant to rival "Millionaires' Row" on Fifth Avenue. The house was palatial, standing four stories high and 224 feet wide. It included twelve rooms in all: two banquet halls, a ballroom, half a dozen bedrooms and bathrooms, and an English basement. Its exterior was made of red brick, stone, and mahogany and embellished with carvings of flowers, vines, and Greek deities. From its stained-glass windows, sunrooms, and projecting balconies it overlooked sheep grazing in the Central Park meadow. Elias had been fascinated by the park since she had first visited New York and had dreamed of taking up residence along its border. Her new address was among the city's white elite, which meant that extra steps had to be taken to conceal her race and affiliation with Platt.

After moving in, Elias left the house only for emergencies, and on those occasions she rode in a covered carriage and wore a veil over her face. She turned the basement of her house into a medical suite equipped with a dentist's chair and surgical tools so that all her checkups and teeth cleanings could be done in-house.

Hoping to preempt anyone becoming privy to the fact that they were living next to a wealthy black woman, she propagated false rumors about her ethnicity. At first, word was spread that she was Sicilian. Elias hired a young Italian man to come to her house and give her language lessons, but before long she started an affair with him. After a few weeks, she became paranoid that he was plotting to murder her for her money after reading a similar plot in a dime novel and fired him. Afterward, she switched to Spanish lessons and began telling people she was Cuban.

She assembled a team of servants for her home that included a black doorman, a French maid, a Senegalese maid, two Japanese butlers, a Chinese cook, and a full-time coach driver. As her neighbors watched her assortment of servants come to and from the house, she became the envy of the block. Foreign domestics were the latest trend in New York high society. At swanky dinner parties and teas thrown by New York's plutocrats, it was not uncommon to hear rich women boast that they had hired help from Germany or Sweden.

Though Elias was unable to show herself in front of her rich neighbors, she still felt compelled to compete with them. Shortly after moving in, she hired a fitness instructor after hearing that a neighbor's wife had gotten her weight down to 84 pounds and became determined to surpass that mark. She also spent thousands of dollars every month draping herself in pearls, diamonds, and furs.

Her extravagance, however, did nothing to cure the loneliness she experienced in her gilded jail. The white elite in the city were a social and tight-knit group. They traveled together, threw parties for one another aboard their yachts and in the ballrooms of their mansions. Elias, as a monied black woman, however, was forced to become a recluse, fearing what might happen if she was discovered living among them.

She had no friends other than Platt and could only watch men and women go by in the park from a seat in her window, never able to walk the promenades herself.

She sought refuge in reading and collected books to help pass the time. One day while reading about the Egyptian ruler Cleopatra, she had an epiphany. Similarities between their lives began to appear to her. As a girl, Cleopatra was exiled by her family. As a woman, she was able to return to rule through an alliance with a powerful older man, Rome's ruler, Julius Caesar. Perhaps, Elias thought, if she remade herself and her surroundings in Cleopatra's image, her home could become a palace, not a prison.

Elias charged her most trusted servant, a slight Japanese man with a thin mustache named Kato, with shopping for the items needed to transform her home. After a frenzy of effort, the walls and windows of the mansion were draped with satin and silk. The rooms were outfitted with perfumed pillows and chaises for Elias to lie on while her servants fed and fanned her with feather fans. She had Kato purchase a fountain that spouted scented water and installed it in her bedroom after reading that Cleopatra had had such an apparatus. When she was bored, she would clap her hands and order her servants to put on Egyptian period costumes and dance for her.

The pageant only minimally eased her malaise. She

was the wealthy mistress of a powerful man, and with her investments and gifts from Platt she was worth close to a million herself. Save for Mary Ellen Pleasant in California, she was most likely the richest black woman in the United States. Yet because of her race she could not even leave her home. She began to think that perhaps she could find freedom if she could make herself white.

"When I was first called upon by this woman I was impressed by her desire to look as much like a white woman as possible," recalled Dr. Edward P. Robinson, a "beauty doctor" Elias hired in 1900. When Robinson first met with Elias in her home, he told her that he couldn't change her tan complexion or her curly hair, but he could give her a new nose, noting that "her nose was typically African as it was depressed at the bridge and spread all over the face." Robinson made eight house calls at $100 ($1,372) apiece to work on Elias.

It's not known what treatments he performed, but it was popular at the time to use paraffin wax to create a structure on the inside of the nostrils to project the tip of the nose outward. Such a treatment could be effective but needed to be redone on a monthly basis and was known to cause difficulty breathing. Nonetheless, after the treatment, Elias's nose was more pronounced. "Ms. Elias now has a perfect type of Grecian nose," the beauty doctor boasted.

After altering her nose, she searched for an expert to change her hair and hired a hairdresser who claimed she could make her locks straight. Elias was instructed to shave her head bald and apply an elixir to her scalp.

The new hair, she was told, would grow in without kinks. However, when it started to grow again, it was as curly as before. Elias, who was left nearly bald, was forced to don wigs after that. She consoled herself by purchasing hairpieces made of Spanish hair that cost upward of several hundred dollars each.

She hoped she would have better results with her complexion. She found a man who claimed he could lighten her skin by applying a mask to her face for thirty days. When it was removed, he told her, her skin would be alabaster white. When she removed the mask, her skin color was unchanged, and by then the salesman had skipped town with the $1,000 ($13,726) she had paid him.

Elias was devastated. The night she removed the mask, she sent a servant to purchase a bucket of possum stew and some liquor that she called "nigger gin" from one of the city's black establishments. When the servant returned, she ate the stew by scooping it from the bucket with her hands while sobbing.

After the meal, she got drunk and began to dance a jig, ordering the staff to join her. She carried on well into the night, until she finally passed out and went to sleep.

The days were mostly the same after that. She would get worked up about something, only to sink into depression and drunkenness when the excitement wore off, and she realized she could escape neither her blackness nor the walls of her mansion.

A New Century

*Success is to be measured not
so much by the position that one
has reached in life as by the
obstacles which he has overcome.*
—BOOKER T. WASHINGTON

13

Last Days of
Mary Ellen Pleasant

In 1892, when she was seventy-seven years old, Mary Ellen Pleasant purchased a ranch in California's Sonoma Valley. The grounds of her new home spanned more than 900 acres and were set against a backdrop of green mountains. The property had acres of crops and pastures, a lake, a horse-racing track, a vineyard, and several guesthouses. There she spent $50,000 ($1.5 million) to build a mansion after spending $100,000 ($3 million) to purchase the property from John Drummond, a famous California winemaker. She built it to resemble the mansions on southern plantations, with a wraparound porch and balcony held up by white pillars, where she was often perched in a rocking chair, enjoying the cool breezes of the California wine country.

Her ranch was her most public display of her wealth, and she used it to send up her critics. The papers had refused to call her by her given name since her streetcar trial, referring to her in print not as Mary Ellen but as "Mammy." She hated the epithet and returned letters addressed to Mammy Pleasant without opening them. She had been born free in the North, but the race-baiting journalism spread rumors that she was a southern slave or voodoo priestess from New Orleans. "Some people have reported that I was born in slavery, but as a matter of fact, I was born in Philadelphia," she said. Her plantation-style estate was perhaps a way of having a laugh at her detractors.

In 1892, as she was preparing to spend her first summer at her new home, she received a telegram from the estate of the former California governor, Newton Booth. He and Pleasant had remained fond of each other after he was elected governor of California and had kept in contact over the many years after he had left her house for the governor's mansion in Sacramento. The envelope that was delivered to Pleasant contained a message inside: Booth was dead.

The letter said that one of Booth's last requests had been that she attend his funeral. Booth's death hit Pleasant just as hard as the deaths of her husbands had. She had met Frederick Douglass and John Brown and rubbed shoulders with the millionaires of San Francisco, but she believed that Booth was the most brilliant man she ever met.

At Sacramento City Cemetery, Booth was laid to rest in front of hundreds of friends and mourners. The cemetery was canopied with trees and cherry blossoms. Booth was buried in a plot underneath a tree with red blooms on its branches. As Booth's pallbearers carried his coffin to his grave, Pleasant followed behind them with tears streaming down her face. She shook so heavily with sobs as they lowered Booth into the ground that she had to be escorted out of the cemetery. After the funeral, she went to stay at Thomas Bell's mansion. Bell's wife, Teresa, decided to spend the summer at Pleasant's ranch, leaving Pleasant and Thomas to run their mansion and the staff.

At 8:30 p.m. on October 15, 1892, Thomas retired to his bedroom on the third floor of the house. Shortly afterward, Pleasant retired to her own room. At 10:30, after a loud crash, one of the servants discovered Thomas unconscious on the ground floor of the house, having fallen twenty feet from the top of the stairs. Doctors were immediately called, but he never regained consciousness and died at 1:30 a.m. The coroner came to the house to question Pleasant, and Bell's son, Thomas Frederick Bell Jr., who was also in the house when Thomas Bell fell from the stairs. Teresa rushed back from Sonoma Valley after her husband's death. "Mr. Bell had been ailing for about two weeks now, and had been in bed since last Monday," Pleasant told the inspector. "He was badly run down, the doctor said, and besides he had trouble with his skin, that just kept him in torture." The coroner questioned the servants at the house and the doctors who had treated him after the fall. After examining Bell's body and reviewing his interview notes, the coroner ruled Bell's death an accident.

Journalists showed up at the house almost immediately after Bell's death. In headlines, they dubbed the mansion "The House of Mystery" and implied that Pleasant had killed Bell. Pleasant wasn't shy about pushing back. "Of course we don't know just how the accident happened, nobody does," the seventy-eight-year-old Pleasant explained. "But we think Mr. Bell may have been dazed when he started down to the kitchen. I think he got to the bottom of the upper flight and then fell over the railing from the first step. The railing is low, and it would be easy to fall from the stairs."

Bell was buried in a cemetery on top of a hill in the west of San Francisco. His estate, which consisted of railroad stock, mining claims, and about $1 million in cash, was valued at $30 million ($827 million). Bell left a third of it to Teresa and stipulated that the estate pay her a monthly allowance of $5,000 ($68,630) to care for their children. The courts later lowered that amount to $2,000 ($27,452).

Before Bell died, Pleasant asked Bell not to put her in his will, for she felt that he had paid her fairly when he was alive. She didn't need anything else; she had her own fortune, which included real estate, boardinghouses, stocks, and cash, and she had a net worth close to a million dollars. She had been hounded by the press for much of her life, and she knew that her name appearing in Bell's will would only lead to scandal.

After Bell's death, Pleasant retired to her ranch in the Sonoma Valley. There she was frequently ill and bedridden. Visitors often came to see her and sent her flowers. "My bedroom looks like a florist shop," she remarked from her bed.

In the years after Bell's death, Frederick and Teresa mismanaged and bickered over his estate. They drained the accounts by spending and bumbling the investments Bell had left them. In 1897, as the estate was running out of money, Frederick took aim at Pleasant. He filed a lawsuit against her, claiming that she had mismanaged his father's estate and insinuating that she had killed Bell by pushing him down the stairs. Pleasant was eighty-three and ailing when Frederick came after her. "This suit has been brought by Fred because some enemies of ours have urged him on, and his action is too shameful to speak about," she told reporters. Having burned through his father's money, Frederick laid claim to Pleasant's, alleging that she had amassed her fortune by stealing from his father. "Thousands of dollars were being pilfered by Pleasant, a mammy in disguise," he said. He asserted that Pleasant's personal property, which he valued at $200,000 ($5.8 million), including an expensive jewelry collection, had been bought with money that had belonged to Thomas Bell.

The case divided the city, with African Americans siding with the elderly Pleasant and her claim that her money, property, and possessions were her own. Whites sided with Frederick's contention that her million-dollar fortune was ill-gotten.

Teresa stayed loyal to Pleasant throughout the trial. In 1894, at eighty years of age, Pleasant had signed her estate over to Teresa. Her health failing, and with no heirs, she wanted Teresa to have the property and keep it away from Fred. During the trial, she and Teresa holed up at the Sonoma Valley estate. Teresa kept her young children there, where they rode horses and played in the orchards. "The girls think of nothing but horses and riding," she wrote in her journal. As Fred's case got under way, Teresa feared that Pleasant was going to lose everything. It had probably been a good idea to sign the estate over to her. "M.P. is out looking for bills in the Fred Bell case. I am in a state of dread," she wrote in her journal. Three days later, Pleasant lifted Teresa's spirits by buying her a fancy French hat. "It was quite an event. I have not had one in years!" Teresa recalled, remembering that her spirits had been momentarily lifted. In 1898, she returned the ownership of the ranch to Pleasant so she could take a loan out against it to cover her legal bills.

In April 1899, Pleasant and Teresa got into a fight. One afternoon, a neighbor came over to ask Pleasant to repay a loan he had made to her. Short on cash, Teresa told her not to pay him, but Pleasant insisted on doing so. "I have plenty more money," she told Teresa. Teresa retorted angrily that Pleasant was repaying loans and still hadn't deeded the estate back to her. "You black-mailer!" she shrieked. "I have a history of your evil deeds and I will mail them to the Bancroft library!" "You are a thief! You stole an armchair from my house on Clara

Street!" Pleasant snapped back. The fight escalated into a screaming match, and both women called the police. When the police arrived, they told the women that they would have to resolve their grievance in the civil courts and left.

The next day the dejected Pleasant locked herself in the bathroom. Teresa smashed in the door and told her to leave. Pleasant packed two trunks with her things and departed the house. "She was snarling like a mad dog," Teresa wrote in her diary. "I am glad, very glad, to go," Pleasant said as she left. A crowd had gathered in the street to witness what was going on, and Teresa took pleasure as they watched "the great Mary E. Pleasant" being humbled.

Pleasant was not so easily defeated. She still had the deeds to the estate and the mansion in the city. After she was thrown out of the house, her creditors attempted to foreclose on her assets. However, they found that her assets were so entangled with Teresa's that it would have been impossible to get anything out of her. Fred wondered if Pleasant had instigated her fight with Teresa and her eviction to foil her creditors.

Pleasant split her time between a cottage and a small house in San Francisco. In 1904, as she became very ill, she went to stay with friends of hers, the Sherwoods, in San Francisco. On the morning of January 11, she was in bed and sensed that death was near. "I do not harbor a vindictive thought against the people who have betrayed my friendship or maligned me, and, in going down to my grave, I forgive them all," she said.

"To my enemies, I say nothing, to my friends . . . I say: God bless you all." Her thoughts in her last hours were not of money but of the fights she had waged for freedom. "James made me promise that I would devote a portion of the money he left me to the cause of freeing the slaves," she said. "Before I die I want to let the world know how I tried to keep my promise." In her final moments she asked her friends to sing an old church song. She hummed along and closed her eyes. Then her voice faded out and she died.

Pleasant left behind an estate worth $600,000 ($16.2 million). At her height, she had been worth more than a million dollars. She was buried under the shade of a big tree in a green meadow in a cemetery in Napa County, California.

14

The Most Powerful
Black Man Alive

At the turn of the century, Robert Reed Church was sixty years old. He now walked with a cane. His eyes were still fiery and bloodshot, and he remained fearless and quick-tempered. A decade earlier, in 1889, he had begun to draw up plans for a park and arena for black citizens in Memphis. As their construction neared completion, he wondered how white Memphis would react to his project. His life had been filled with attacks by Confederates, racist police officers, and segregationists for daring to strive as a black person. Many winters earlier, he had been pelted with rocks by racists for having had the audacity as a black man to be the only man in Memphis with a sled. What would they do when he opened a $100,000 ($2.9 million) arena?

As a young man, he had dealt with white men with his fist and gun; now, gray and wrinkled, he decided to exert a skill he had acquired with age: diplomacy. In 1900, a group of ex–Confederate soldiers decided to throw a reunion for Confederate veterans in Memphis. As they struggled to raise $80,000 to build a temporary auditorium in which to hold the affair, they received an unexpected donation of $1,000 ($29,245) from Church, a former slave. "I never gave a cent in my life, so cheerfully or gladly as I gave that check to the veterans' entertainment fund," he said afterward. He had learned that goodwill could be bought when he had helped bail out Memphis from bankruptcy. He hoped that $1,000 would be enough to protect his arena from the same resistance as his pool hall, which a white mob had burned down when he was a young entrepreneur.

Church Park and Auditorium opened a few weeks after the Confederate reunion, without incident. The 1,200-seat auditorium had two levels, including a balcony. The stage was covered by a drop curtain that had a painting of the burning *Bulletin No. 2* on it. Behind the curtain was a dark-stained wooden stage with a bandstand. The auditorium sat on a four-acre park ringed by flower gardens with carnival rides, an outdoor theater, gazebos, and orange trees. Peacocks roamed its grounds, spreading their colorful tails to the delight of visitors. He put on concerts with big bands. Eventually he called his park a "resort for colored people." Since he had built the park without loans or partners, black newspapers began to refer to him as the wealthiest black man in America. Church and the park's African American visitors were left alone. It seemed that Church's $1,000 donation bought him and Memphis' African American population enough room to enjoy the paradise he had built for them.

TO SEGREGATIONIST DEMOCRATS AND WHITE NATIONALISTS IN Memphis, Church's overture may have appeared to be political surrender, but in fact it was exactly the opposite. In 1900, shortly after the opening of his park, Church became a delegate to the Republican National Convention. There he nominated Theodore Roosevelt for vice president and William McKinley for president. He donated $5,000 ($146,225) to the ticket, making him one of the largest contributors to the campaign and winning him favor with the White House. Church's younger self, an enslaved boy in the Mississippi delta, might have found his current station in life incredible. He was now a millionaire, the richest black man in the country, with a line to the president. Church became acquainted with Booker T. Washington around 1900, when Washington was starting an organization called the National Negro Business League, a black business network and think tank. Church was one of the first to join. Beyond sharing an interest in black entrepreneurship, Church and Washington didn't see eye to eye. They "vehemently disagreed on everything." Church sent his children to boarding school, to college at Oberlin, and donated to black schools. Having been deprived of an education himself, he resented Washington's focus on "manual labor" instead of "education and ballots." Their differences aside, the two became allies, and Church invited Washington to be one of the speakers at Church Auditorium. When McKinley was assassinated in 1901 and Roosevelt became president, Church was among the group that encouraged President Roosevelt to invite Booker T. Washington to the White House, as an olive branch to black America. After the death of his friend Frederick Douglass in 1895, Washington had assumed the mantle of the most prominent and influential black leader and activist in the country. On May 2, 1901, Roosevelt, heeding the calls from Washington's supporters, invited him to dinner at the White House. For men like Church, who had been born into slavery and lived in a segregated South, the symbolism of seeing a black man dine in the White House with the president was awe-inspiring.

Church later wrote the president and asked him to give an address to the colored people of Memphis in Church Auditorium.

THE CROWD IN CHURCH AUDITORIUM WAS JUBILANT IN 1902 WHEN President Roosevelt took the stage and stared out at a sea of brown faces. Church sat behind him in a pin-striped suit and a bowler hat, rocking back and forth in his chair and holding his cane in his hands. A brass band played "Dixie," followed by "The Star-Spangled Banner," and then, after speeches from the mayor of Memphis and the governor of Louisiana, Roosevelt took the stage and gave a short speech. Afterward he stood and waved to the crowd as the band played "It'll Be a Hot Time in the Old Town Tonight."

Though not as sensational, the president's address to an all-black audience in a black-owned auditorium in the South was in many ways as much of a milestone as Washington's dinner at the White House. Church was now a power broker politically, socially, and economically.

Church continued his economic ascent, buying buildings in Beale until, by 1906, he owned most of the district. That year he opened a bank in one of the buildings and named it the Solvent Savings Bank & Trust Co. It was a two-story brick building painted white with a plate-glass window. Church, who had for years lent out rolls of cash from behind the bar and in the back rooms of his saloons, was now officially in the bank business as the first black owner of a bank in Memphis. He deposited $25,000 ($671,272) of his own money, and the bank promised to pay 3 percent interest on deposits.

In 1907, the Panic of 1907 started a run on the banks. The unfortunate timing could have ended Church's bank; if all his depositors took out their money at once, it would fail. He staved off a run on the bank by exhibiting stacks of money in the plate-glass window, thus assuring his customers that he was solvent and it was safe to keep their money there. In 1908, when a white bank tried to foreclose on the black Baptist church that Ida B. Wells had attended as a young woman, Church and his bank swooped in and paid off the loan, saving it.

SEVERAL YEARS LATER, IN 1910, ROBERT HEBERTON TERRELL, HIS son-in-law, was nominated to the Washington, D.C., circuit court. When he was confirmed, he became the first black judge in Washington. It was yet another milestone for Church and his family. Risen from bondage, he had become a self-made man, a beloved son of Memphis, a connected political power broker, and the South's first black millionaire.

Church was an old man by then. His hair was white and thinning, and he leaned heavily on his cane to walk. As a young man he had worked around the clock in his saloon, keeping the lights on till the wee hours of the morning. In his last years, he did the same at his bank. Working beside his son Robert Reed Church Jr., the heir of his dynasty, the elder Robert Church spent his entire day in his office at the bank, writing loans and drumming up deposits. Without fail, as the sun set and people took to Beale Street for a night on the town to see W. C. Handy and others perform a new type of music called the blues, they'd see the light on in Bob's office. In the summer of 1912, Church began having heart trouble and was put on bed rest. Fearing the worst, his friends and family members flocked to Memphis to say good-bye. In his final hours, Booker T. Washington went in to see Church. He was the last person to see him alive. In August 1912, Church died of a heart attack. He left behind a wife and five children and an estate worth over a million dollars.

15

"Black Wall Street" Rises

In 1905, W. E. B. Du Bois, then an upstart scholar and activist, organized a summit of black leaders near Niagara Falls. He was backed by Alonzo Herndon, a former slave from Georgia who was now the owner of the country's largest black insurance company, Atlanta Life Insurance.[*] In a hotel room in Fort Erie, Ontario, more than two dozen attendees huddled together and laid out a plan for a movement that countered the overtly conciliatory politics of Booker T. Washington with a call for farm ownership, good jobs, and self-defense from lynching.

As a debate was beginning over the course of black America's future in 1905, an accidental discovery provided an opportunity for many African Americans

---

[*] Herndon later became Atlanta's first black millionaire in the 1920s.

to escape the horrors of lynching and obtain better wages. One afternoon oil was found on a farm owned by a family of Creek Indians just outside Tulsa, Oklahoma. The gusher and the subsequent discovery of other oil deposits in Tulsa created an oil boom in the city. More than a hundred oil companies were set up in Tulsa in response to the discovery. The oil barons and chambers of commerce sent out boosters on trains and traveling publicity teams with bands, Indians in full headgear, and cowboys, including the young Will Rogers, to recruit people to come to Tulsa to work in its oil fields, refineries, and shops to hopefully turn it into a boomtown.

Brown faces were among the first to show up in Tulsa after oil was discovered. When the African Americans arrived, the town was a small village with dirt streets, dotted with tanneries. There were butchers' shops with warm animal carcasses hanging in the windows, mason shops, and a few homes, small churches, and a school in wood-framed buildings. The first years in Tulsa were difficult. The houses had no indoor plumbing system, and the town was hot and humid in the summer months. On hot nights, families often slept on mattresses outside their homes, where they were feasted on by mosquitoes and flies. Outlaws on the backs of horses, wearing cowboy hats, who had been in the city since the end of the war, periodically rode into town to terrorize its new residents, shooting out the windows of homes and churches just for the thrill of it and holding up shops and banks.

Nonetheless, wagons filled to the brim with African Americans, sharecroppers from the South on foot carrying carpetbags, and people on the backs of mules continued to arrive in Tulsa. African Americans from the Deep South flocked to Oklahoma as lynchings, terror, and race crimes worsened in the southern states. They hoped that across the Mississippi they would find a good job in the boomtown. But even in comparatively progressive Oklahoma, they couldn't totally escape racism. The high-paying jobs in the oil fields were off-limits to blacks. Nonetheless, they sent word back home that Tulsa was integrated, safe, and there was plenty of work, even with the prohibition on hiring blacks for oil jobs. Boosters recruited African Americans to Oklahoma, promising them work and security. The immigrants from the South earned the nickname "Exodusters" as they set out for Oklahoma, where they hoped they could, at last, find the Promised Land.

Blacks took jobs in town, working side by side with whites. They worked in the homes of whites as domestics, as well as opened businesses, supervising both black and white employees. In the city's early days, as the spirit of boosterism and unity muted racial tensions, blacks and whites sometimes lived next door to one another, ate at the same restaurants, and allowed their children to play together, as they worked to build the "Magic City," as they liked to call it. Locals labeled the good feelings shared by blacks, whites, Jews, and Indians in early Tulsa "the Tulsa Spirit." African Americans in Tulsa thought the good feelings would last, believing that whites in the city were too preoccupied making money in the oil boom to erect a social racial caste system.

Ottowa W. Gurley took notice of the oil boom in Tulsa from his home in Perry. Soon after the boom began, he sold his land in Perry and moved to Tulsa with his wife, Emma. He was now thirty-five years old and saw an economic opportunity in Tulsa's multiracial population boom. In Tulsa he bought a 40-acre tract of land north of the train station and built a grocery store on a dirt road in the middle of the undeveloped swath of land that sat north of the train tracks that ran across the city. He also forged an informal partnership with another black businessman named John the Baptist Stradford. Stradford was tall and sinewy, with a prominent square jaw and piercing black eyes. Both men, with their families' roots in enslavement, shared a distrust of white people and went by their initials, OW and JB respectively, instead of their first names. It was the custom in the South that men were addressed by their title or surname and boys by their first name. Black adult males were frequently called by their first names by white men as a form of emasculation.

OW was a subscriber to the philosophies of Booker T. Washington, while JB was a follower of the more radical W. E. B. Du Bois. Nonetheless, both believed that the racial harmony in Tulsa was temporary, and the two men began to develop an all-black district in the unincorporated stretch of land north of Tulsa's train station. They subdivided the plots they owned in uptown Tulsa on the north side of a set of railroad tracks into housing and retail lots, alleys and streets that they made available only to other African Americans fleeing the lynchings and terror of the South for the economic opportunity of Tulsa's oil boom. On a long street near the train tracks made of dry dirt and dust Gurley built boarding-houses in square two-story brick structures near his grocery store, naming the street Greenwood Avenue, after the town in Mississippi from which many of his first residents hailed. There he also built a colored school and an African Methodist Episcopal Church. Soon the entire north side of Tulsa was referred to as Greenwood.

Gurley also built three brick apartment buildings as well as five detached homes, which he rented out to blacks. His crowning project was the Gurley Hotel on Greenwood Avenue, which was valued at $55,000 and rivaled the best white hotels in Tulsa. OW and JB both became rich as the oil industry boomed on in Tulsa and hundreds of African Americans emigrated to Greenwood. In 1914, the local black newspaper, the *Muskogee Scimitar*, reported Gurley's net worth to be as much as $150,000 ($3.6 million). He used his wealth to help start a black Masonic lodge in Greenwood and an employment agency, and he contributed to efforts to push back against black voter suppression in the state. Gurley was made a sheriff's deputy by the city of Tulsa and charged with policing the black population in Greenwood. Gurley's wealth and coziness with the white establishment in Tulsa created resentment of him among many black members of society, who saw him as having too much power in Greenwood. Many saw Gurley as an

Uncle Tom. In the *Tulsa Star*, which was operated by a militant black columnist and publisher named A. J. Smitherman, Gurley was pejoratively referred to as the "king" of "little Africa."

Following behind OW and JB, white developers began to buy up plots of land north of the railroad tracks and sell them to blacks. By 1905, the district had attracted a black doctor and a black dentist, who each established practices there. A second school, a newspaper, a Baptist church, and a hardware store were also built. Gurley and Stradford's vision of an all-black district was taking shape. At the same time, informal segregation was occurring in Tulsa as blacks converged to the north of the tracks and whites to the south.

In the morning, dozens of Greenwood residents walked across the train tracks to domestic jobs in Tulsa; the remainder stayed behind, working at the new black businesses that were being developed in Greenwood. Alongside the professional businesses were juke joints, saloons, and gambling houses. Their black proprietors grew rich in Greenwood catering to white men's vices.

When the Oklahoma territory achieved statehood in 1907 and segregationist Democrats, led by the white supremacist Bill "Alfalfa" Murray, took control of all levels of government, they passed laws against interracial marriage and prohibited blacks from working at high-wage jobs. In 1910, one of the first grandfather clauses preventing blacks from voting was passed. As OW and JB watched the state, led by Alfalfa Bill, who was now Speaker of the state house of representatives, enact Jim

Crow laws, they knew they had been right all along not to rely on the Tulsa Spirit.

When blacks moved to Tulsa, they invariably ended up in Greenwood. The district swelled northward, with Gurley and Stradford buying up more land to expand its boundaries. As it grew, the streets filled with doctors' offices, banks, funeral homes, saloons, clubs, and beauty salons. In 1909, Greenwood was annexed by the town of Tulsa, on the other side of the train tracks.

Black farming communities and black districts such as Greenwood existed across the country. In Atlanta, Alonzo Herndon helped found the Sweet Auburn District, an enclave of black politicians, professors, and deans from Spelman and Atlanta universities, and preachers such as Martin Luther King Sr. Tulsa was, however, different from places such as Memphis, Atlanta, Jacksonville, St. Louis, and Chicago; Greenwood was an affluent black enclave in a white city where blacks controlled no political institutions and could rely only on one another to protect themselves from racial hostility. Across the tracks, resentment simmered. There were talks of attacks on Greenwood. Literature was distributed declaring that there had been rapes of white women by black men. Blacks were also intimidated at voting polls. Blacks in Tulsa responded with public protests, raising racial tensions to a boiling point.

Greenwood's population more than quadrupled from 1,959 to 8,000 under Gurley's watch, as African Americans gravitated to the black town, drawn by its promise and prosperity. Greenwood's growth was a source of frustration and paranoia for local whites, as Tulsa's percentage of blacks ticked up from 10 percent to 12 percent and Greenwood's economic prowess grew. Black migrants continued to stream in, and some whites feared they would eventually take over the entire town of Tulsa.

Their fear was perhaps fueled by the militancy of Greenwood's black constituents. Greenwood was equal parts black mecca and Wild West. Both men and women frequently carried pistols with them, and disputes were often settled by street brawls and shootouts. Believing they had left hegemony behind in the South, Greenwood's residents had little tolerance for racial violence. They were quick to respond to attacks or threats from whites with punches or bullets. In one such instance in 1909, J. B. Stradford was walking along Greenwood Avenue when a white deliveryman made a pejorative remark about his dark skin. Stradford jumped on the man and threw him to the ground. He then straddled him and beat him until his face was covered with blood. A group of black men came running up and pulled him off. "If you kill him, they'll mob you," one said. Stradford was charged for the beating but hired an attorney and was acquitted. Later, Stradford was kicked off a train in Oklahoma for riding in the first-class car, having purchased a first-class ticket. He was asked to move to the colored car but refused. He sued in an effort to desegregate Tulsa's train cars but lost in court, to the chagrin of Greenwood's residents. A few months after Stradford's assault case, news of the death of black millionaire Robert Reed Church reached Tulsa; blacks who had known him or known of him mourned the death of the titan. Gurley, with his growing wealth and power, was a logical successor to Church as the South's most powerful black man, but Gurley's interests were local, as he was chiefly concerned with his own fortunes, as well as Greenwood's.

In Oklahoma, the forces of segregation were gaining strength. Housing segregation was legalized, banning blacks from living in white neighborhoods. The segregation of Tulsa, ironically, strengthened Greenwood's black business district. The dollars earned by Greenwood's black professionals as well as the black domestics who made money on the white side of town seemed never to leave Greenwood. Merchants boasted that a black dollar circulated through the black community twenty-six times before it left. As Jim Crow laws were passed throughout the country, the economic effects experienced in Greenwood were replicated, as black communities became economically independent and black merchants and businesses marketed to a captive and loyal market.

Greenwood was thriving as segregation spread across the state and the country. On Thursday nights, Greenwood was the place to be for men and women of color, as well as whites, who would slip across the train tracks without being seen by their neighbors. On Thursdays and Sundays, domestics had the day off, and on Thursday nights they came together to party late into the evening. The cooks, butlers, chauffeurs, and laundresses who worked in the white section of Tulsa took to the streets of Greenwood to dance. The dingy roads, which the white politicians in city hall neglected to pave or light, came alive as vendors lined the sidewalks with stands that offered candy, peaches, and watermelons. Men dressed in navy blue and black suits with off-white shirts and gold pocket watches, and women in silk dresses that hugged their midsections and hips, flowed into the streets as the sun went down. There was no music, no band, just the sound of people's feet sliding on the dirt roads. Together they moved to their own internal rhythm, hollering, shaking, swirling down the streets in a communal strut like the second line of a New Orleans parade. "It was like a pantomime, people just moving up and down," remembered the historian John Hope Franklin, who grew up in Greenwood. "They were going in and out of restaurants and they were just there to be seen. They were dressed in their finest, and they looked beautiful to me."

Greenwood was not the richest black town in the United States, not even close. Annie Malone's industrializing St. Louis, Bob Church's blues-filled Memphis, and Alonzo Herndon's Atlanta, filled with black colleges and businesses, all had a much larger black professional class than Greenwood did. What made Greenwood special was that it was a place a sharecropper, an ordinary person, could go to and have a respectable life, find decent-paying work, and hope for a better life for his children. With oilmen relocating to Tulsa, the resulting high demand for domestics enabled blacks to attain

unheard-of wages. Maids earned $20 to $25 ($500 to
$625) a week; chauffeurs earned $15 ($375); garden-
ers made $20 ($500); janitors, shoe shiners, and porters
earned around $10 ($250). Domestics made up almost
two-thirds of Greenwood's population, the remainder
being professionals and business owners, whom the
maids and chauffeurs hoped their children could imi-
tate one day. The children of Greenwood's professionals attended Columbia Law School, Oberlin College,
the Hampton Institute, the Tuskegee Institute, Spelman
College, and Atlanta University. Greenwood's culture
prided itself on education; the area had one of the lowest black illiteracy rates in the country and a high school
graduation rate above 50 percent. This was unheard-of
in other areas of the country. Tulsa was indeed a Magic
City for African Americans.

THE STORIES OF GREENWOOD'S PROSPERITY BECAME LEGEND IN
black America. Annie Malone set up an office to sell her
hair products in the enclave and it became known as one
of the country's most economically stable black districts.
Booker T. Washington gave Greenwood a new name, "Negro Wall Street" (which later became "Black Wall Street").

AS GREENWOOD GREW PROSPEROUS, GURLEY, ITS ARCHITECT AND
lawman, continued to be accused of being too moder-

ate and racially conciliatory. That changed for a night when he had an encounter with three white men in Tulsa. That cool evening in the winter of 1916, he was forced to confront the race problem when it arrived at his doorstep. Three white men entered the Gurley hotel and encountered O. W. Gurley's wife, Emma, on the second floor of the hotel. "We're looking for good time girls," one of the men told Emma. Moments later, OW arrived to find the men harassing his wife. "What is your business here?" Gurley asked them. The men didn't answer, and Emma spoke up and told OW what the men had said. Gurley rushed at the men and knocked all three of them to the ground with a series of punches. The men climbed to their feet and ran toward the stairs to escape but were sent tumbling down them by kicks from OW as he gave chase. At the bottom of the stairs Gurley tried to get the men to stand and fight, but instead they bolted for the exit and ran away into the night. Beating three white men made Gurley a hero in Greenwood, but it begged the question: if the racial conservative Gurley had resorted to using violence against whites, was there any hope for lasting peace between Greenwood and white Tulsa?

16

Battle for Hair Supremacy

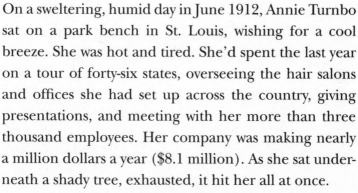

On a sweltering, humid day in June 1912, Annie Turnbo sat on a park bench in St. Louis, wishing for a cool breeze. She was hot and tired. She'd spent the last year on a tour of forty-six states, overseeing the hair salons and offices she had set up across the country, giving presentations, and meeting with her more than three thousand employees. Her company was making nearly a million dollars a year ($8.1 million). As she sat underneath a shady tree, exhausted, it hit her all at once.

She was always working. There in the park in Missouri, she was in the middle of pitching to a few dozen women who were interested in becoming sales agents for her company, Poro. She told the women that her sales agents were the evangelists of Poro and Poro women were examples for other black women, who "spread the gospel of personal appearance." When she finished, several women approached her to ask questions about possible employment. One woman was out of work after she had injured her leg in a furniture factory where she had been employed. Another woman had been taking care of her infant niece since her brother died and was looking for work she could do from home. A woman who was a principal at a local school was intrigued. She said she was looking for a new career. Annie signed several saleswomen that afternoon, expanding her army of Poro representatives. After she finished signing them up, she closed her eyes, leaned back, and dabbed sweat from her face with a handkerchief. As she started to relax, she heard a voice behind her: "Nothing cools like lemonade." When she opened her eyes, she saw a man standing in front of her, smiling and holding a glass of lemonade. He introduced himself as Aaron Malone.

Aaron Malone was a traveling Bible salesman. He had big brown eyes, caramel-colored skin, and short, straight hair. "You picked a good time to start your company," he told Annie. She agreed. As the Reconstruction era was replaced by Jim Crow and blacks were excluded from white shops and sections of town, a powerful black economy was emerging. Excluded from white institutions, blacks sought black-owned businesses and built all-black communities in which to spend their hard-earned dollars.

It had been a whirlwind since the World's Fair. Annie had opened Poro College, a training center for hairstylists, built a sales force of thousands, and franchised hundreds of beauty shops. She hardly had time to enjoy or even count her money, as she was always on the road.

"Do you employ men?" Aaron asked with a smile. "No, but I believe many men help their wives who are Poro agents," she told him. Still smiling, Aaron rubbed his chin as if he were thinking. "Well," he finally said, "if I want a job I guess I'll have to marry the boss."

Annie was flattered but too busy to date or be courted. Aaron was persistent. He began showing up at Annie's presentations to flirt with her. Soon they began dating and then became engaged.

AS ANNIE WAS FINDING LOVE AND ENJOYING BEING A MILLION-aire, Madam C. J. Walker's business was struggling and her marriage was on the rocks. The business was making a little over $10,000 ($250,000) a year selling hair products through the mail and franchising beauty salons. The Walkers' share of profits was enough for them to purchase better clothes, housing, and transportation but nowhere close to Annie's nearly million-dollar market share. After leaving Denver in 1906, Walker had set up shop in Pittsburgh for a few years before moving to Indianapolis, Indiana, in 1910.

Madam, who had fully expected to be neck and neck with Annie at that point, blamed much of the company struggle on her husband, who seemed to be more interested in fronting a prestigious company than running a business. He often failed to fulfill orders, came up with products that nobody would buy, and mismanaged the company's money. He also drank too much and flirted openly with other women. Madam moved to minimize his role in the company by moving him from the manager's office to the road. Walker was a natural salesman, and sending him on the road to drum up business strengthened sales and allowed her to take the reins of management. It came with one risk, though: spending nights alone could lead to his being unfaithful. It was a risk she had to take to keep him out of the day-to-day business.

As she began to take over, Madam made plans to restructure the entire company. She wanted to build a factory and mass-produce her Wonderful Hair Grower and other products instead of making them in small batches on her stove or outsourcing her production to another manufacturer.

Shortly after they arrived in Indianapolis, the Walkers bought a home on the north side of the city, in a middle-class black enclave of shop owners, grocers, and domestics. She purchased a two-story, three-bedroom brick home at 420 North West Street with a balcony on the second floor facing the street for $3,500 ($87,330). After purchasing the home, Madam renovated it by adding two additional bedrooms and bathrooms and placed an ad in the local newspaper for borders to supplement her income. "Four congenial lady roomers, teachers preferred, modern house, 640 N. West Street," it read.

After moving in two boarders and finishing the renovations, she threw a housewarming party. More than a hundred guests attended, bringing gifts. The interior of the house was decorated with cut flowers and palm trees and the Walkers hired a harpist to provide background music for the gathering. After introducing herself to her neighbors and getting settled in Indianapolis, Madam began rebuilding her company. Among the attendees at the housewarming was George Knox, the publisher of *The Freeman*, the largest black newspaper in Indiana. He and Madam struck up a friendship. Knox was a loyal friend and enthusiastic booster of those he considered to be in his inner circle. Shortly after the two became friends, Knox became Madam's most enthusiastic advocate, printing articles about her in his paper and taking creative license to publicize her wealth and success.

In 1912, Madam went on the road to raise $50,000 ($1.2 million) to build a factory. Staying in colored boardinghouses in North Carolina, Virginia, New York, California, and Missouri, she visited black industrialists, lawyers, and doctors, trying to get them to invest in her idea. She returned from her trip unsuccessful and decided to put up her house as collateral for a small loan to build a factory in a brick building down the street.

As Madam was restructuring, Poro remained the dominant brand of black women's hair care products. Madam knew if she were to compete with Annie, it would be not with superior hair products but in the marketing and branding.

At the time, Booker T. Washington was the most famous black person in America. He was a friend of the black industrialist Alonzo Herndon and the late Robert Reed Church. He was also the head of the Tuskegee Institute and the founder, along with Andrew Carnegie, of the National Negro Business League, a preeminent organization for African American entrepreneurs. Madam believed that if she could win an endorsement from Washington, her brand would vault to the top.

Winning an endorsement from Washington would not be easy. He despised black hair care and beauty products, believing that they encouraged the imitation of whiteness. "I have come to view with alarm . . . hair straightening advertising," he once wrote to a black newspaper, imploring it not to carry black hair and makeup ads. At the Tuskegee Institute, he banned makeup for the Indian and black students.

In 1912, Madam wrote to Washington, asking for permission to sell her hair care products at the agricultural convention in Tuskegee. Washington rejected the idea, scolding her for wanting to sell hair care products to poor black farmers. "I do not feel that a visit to our conference would offer the opportunity which you desire," he wrote back in diplomatic but cold prose. Madam went there anyway.

The week of the convention, she showed up on the porch of Washington's house at the Tuskegee Institute, hoping to get him to reconsider. The house sat on a half-acre lawn across from the institute. It was made of red brick and built in the Queen Anne style, with two balconies and a porch that wrapped around the house. Madam knocked on the front door and asked to talk to Washington in person. Washington refused to speak with her and dispatched his assistant to deal with her instead. Madam delivered a letter via his assistant asking that he reconsider and let her speak at the convention. Later that day, perhaps won over by her persistence, he sent word back to her that she could speak for ten minutes but could do no selling.

She spoke the first night of the convention about having risen from the sharecropping fields to start a hair business. Few, including Washington, were impressed with her oration. According to legend, she did not give up. She went back to Washington's home a second day and she won him over by demonstrating her products on his female friends and relatives, shampooing and styling their hair. In the end, he allowed Walker to sell her products to attendees at the remainder of the convention. Perhaps he was warming to the idea of black beauty products.

Before she left Tuskegee, Madam installed an agent in the region to continue selling her products. She selected Dora Larrie, a thirtysomething understudy of hers in Indianapolis. A few months after Dora was set up, Mr. Walker began an affair with her. For several months, the two met in hotels in Alabama. Together they conspired to pull the same trick that Madam had on Annie Malone: they decided they would knock off Madam's products and start their own line together. Once they were off the ground, he would leave Madam and marry Dora. Shortly thereafter, Dora stopped work-ing for Madam and moved to Atlanta, Georgia, to get started on the new venture.

When Madam discovered their plans and their affair, she was furious. Madam, who often carried a revolver in her purse for protection, contemplated killing Mr. Walker but thought better of it. Instead, she cut off access to their bank accounts and hired a lawyer to begin divorce proceedings.

In 1912, Madam attended a conference of the Negro Business League in Chicago, a convention for black entrepreneurs. More than two hundred African American businessmen and -women were expected to be in attendance. Along with Madam, the convention was attended by her fellow Hoosier George Knox.

On Thursday morning, the first day of the conven-tion, Booker T. Washington introduced Anthony Over-ton, the founder and owner of the Overton Hygienic Manufacturing Company. His company was "the larg-est Colored manufacturing enterprise in the United States," Washington noted. Overton was a titan. He had been born a slave in Louisiana in 1865. After Emanci-pation, he and his family had moved to Topeka, Kan-sas. In 1881, Overton opened a grocery store. He used the profits from his store to put himself through law school at Washburn College in Topeka. In 1892, he was elected a municipal judge in Topeka, becoming one of only a handful of black jurists in the country. In 1898, after he and his family saved $2,000 ($60,000), he moved to Kansas City, Missouri, and opened the

Overton Hygienic Manufacturing Company, an outfit that produced and sold baking powder. Later he moved the company to Chicago and began selling cosmetics and toiletries as well. He started his company with "less than $2,000," Washington bragged as he stood next to Overton. Overton was a fair-skinned black man with a toothbrush mustache, serious eyes, big ears, and hair parted in the center and shellacked straight. As he took the convention floor, he looked out into the audience where Madam was sitting and told his fellow entrepreneurs that his key to success had been focusing on black consumers. "When we added our line of toilet articles, we placed colored girls' pictures on our Talcum Powder, Hair Pomades, and other toilet articles." A smattering of applause and cheers came from the crowd. He continued, telling them that his "High-Brown" face powder was his company's best seller. On the top of each box was an empty circle where the model should have gone. The space, he said, was reserved "for the most beautiful colored woman in the United States, which we propose to put on the box later as soon as we find her." Nods, applause, and laughter came from the audience.

Washington opened up the floor for questions. George Knox stood, ostensibly to ask a question. When Washington called upon him, he redirected attention to his friend Madam C. J. Walker. "I arise to ask this convention for a few minutes of its time to hear a remarkable woman," he began. "She is the woman who gave $1,000 to the Young Men's Christian Association of Indianapolis. Madam Walker, the lady I refer to, is the manufacturer of hair goods and preparations." Washington let Knox finish before telling him that his intervention was off subject. He then called on the next questioner. Walker and Knox were crushed by Washington's response; they had been sure that the mention of Walker's donation would have curried favor with Washington; instead, it seemed to have had the opposite effect, appearing self-congratulatory and self-promotional.

On Friday, the final day of the convention, Madam decided that she would get Washington to listen to her one way or another. As Reverend E. M. Griggs, the head of the Farmers and Citizens Savings Bank of Palestine, Texas, was wrapping up his speech, Madam seized the floor. "Surely you are not going to shut the door in my face," she said, staring at Washington, daring him to stop her from speaking. Heads turned in her direction as she locked eyes with Washington. "I went into a business that is despised, that is criticized and talked about by everybody, the business of growing hair," she began. She related her annual earnings, letting the crowd know that she was making $10,000 a year ($252,248). She listed the properties she owned, including her home in Indiana. "I have built my own factory on my own ground, 38 by 208 feet. I employ in that factory several people, including a bookkeeper, a stenographer, a cook and a house girl," she continued. "I own my own automobile." She concluded by revealing an aspiration of opening a beauty school in Africa: "By the help of God and the cooperation of my people in this country, I am going to build a Tuskegee Institute in Africa!" Her attempt at impressing Washington with a demonstration of wealth and flattery hung in the air as she waited for him to respond. "The next banker to address us is Mr. W. W. Hadnott, of the Prudential Savings Bank of Birmingham, Alabama," Washington said, resuming the scheduled activities as if Walker's outburst had never occurred.

Madam and Knox returned to Indianapolis defeated, but Knox tried to put a positive spin on the events, taking creative license, as he often did, to help his friend. He wrote that Madam had been one of the "big hits" of the conference. She "at once impresses an audience with the fact that she stands for concrete achievements rather than brilliance of oratory." As far as anyone in Indiana knew, Madam had been received warmly by Booker T. Washington. But she would have to keep working if she wanted a genuine endorsement.

A little over a week after the conference, Madam filed for divorce from Mr. Walker in Indianapolis. Their marriage was not legal, as Madam had never divorced her previous husband, and she left Mr. Walker with little ground to stand on to pursue her assets. In October 1912, their divorce became final and Mr. Walker was left with nothing.

Mr. Walker and Dora Larrie's new venture, the Walker-Larrie Company, sputtered in marketing its hair products. They married in 1913, and Dora dubbed herself Madam C. J. Walker; then she broke off her relationship with C. J. and pushed him out of their new venture. "We were not married for long before I discovered that she did not love me, but that she only wanted the Madam title and the formula," he lamented.

Divorced from the first Madam Walker and estranged from the second, C. J. struggled to make ends meet. In 1914, he printed a public apology to the original Madam Walker, hoping she would take him back. "I let drink and this designing of evil women come between us," he wrote. Madam wrote to him through her lawyer, suggesting that he relocate overseas and start his own hair company and including $35 ($900) in the letter. "Madam does not understand why you don't go to Key West, Cuba or some other place in which she has few agents," the lawyer wrote, counseling him to "Keep sober and build a big business." In her heart, Madam hoped he would be able to pull himself together one day. Instead, he continued to write her, asking her to reconcile or give him money or a job. Any chance at reconciliation died when he started selling the formula for Wonderful Hair Grower to knockoff companies. Nonetheless, he never stopped writing Madam to try to win her back. He was "writing these lines with tears dripping from my eyes," he wrote in one of his many letters.

AS MADAM WAS MOVING ON FROM HER BROKEN MARRIAGE TO MR. Walker, Annie Turnbo and Aaron Eugene Malone were preparing to get married in St. Louis.* Aaron was a teacher and salesman with a modest income. By 1914, Annie, on the other hand, was worth between $1.5 million and $3 million (between $36.4 million and $72.8 million) and the head of a business empire with more than four thousand agents in forty-six states, as well as Jamaica, Trinidad, Cuba, West Africa, and the Philippines. She lived in a mansion managed by two maids. Her home had twenty-six rooms, many of which she let out to boarders. It sat just above the site of the World's Fair at Forest Park on the west end of St. Louis.

In the fall, Annie and Aaron were married in Annie's palatial home in front of more than a thousand of her friends, family members, and employees. She was smitten with Aaron. Shortly after they married, she put all her assets, including the house, into both their names and made him the chief executive officer of Poro.

In 1916, the Malones broke ground on a new headquarters that would span nearly an entire two-acre city block of St. Louis and employ more than two hundred people. The large four-story rectangular brick building would include a college with dozens of classrooms, meeting rooms, a dining hall, and a dormitory. It would also include a factory, where Poro products would be made, and a greenhouse, where the herbs for the products and the vegetables and fruits for the dining hall would be grown.

---

* Aaron Malone would be Annie's second husband. She was married to a man named Nelson Pope from 1903 to 1907. The relationship fell apart when Pope tried to take over the management of her business and ended in divorce.

AS ANNIE WAS EXPANDING HER BEAUTY BUSINESS, MADAM BEGAN to focus less on her hair care business and more on real estate and cementing herself as a member of the black elite. In 1912, she purchased a brownstone town house in Harlem in the northern part of Manhattan, hoping to soon relocate from Indianapolis to the glitz and glamour of Manhattan, where she might better enjoy her wealth. "I am preparing myself so that when this hair business falls to the ground I will have an income and I won't have to come down," she said in 1912. Madam continued to spend, buying a Cole touring car, the top luxury vehicle on the market. Her daughter, A'Lelia Walker, who Madam was grooming to take over the business one day, spent thousands of dollars on pearls, gold, and clothing. Freeman Briley Ransom, Madam's business manager, was worried about the Walkers' financial habits. "I want you to join me in urging Madam . . . to bank a large portion of her money to the end that it be accumulating and drawing interest for possible rainy days," he pleaded to A'Lelia in letters.

Madam's new, lavish lifestyle ate away at her profits, but it also raised her profile. She was not the first rich African American, but she was perhaps the first to be both brazenly wealthy and openly black. Hannah Elias and Jeremiah Hamilton were both incredibly rich, but they tried to distance themselves from other African Americans. Dr. James McCune Smith was at least as wealthy as Madam, but he detested materialism and lived a minimalistic lifestyle. Robert Reed Church, the country's most well-known black millionaire, had died a few months prior. The black society pages reported on Madam's cars, houses, and jewelry. It made people wonder, how much money does she have? Is she a millionaire?

In the summer of 1913, Madam heard that Booker T. Washington was coming to Indianapolis for the grand opening of the new YMCA, and she invited him to stay at her house in Indianapolis during his visit. To her surprise, he accepted. When Washington arrived at the train station, she had a car and chauffeur waiting for him and had informed the newspapers of his arrival. Reporters were stationed at her door, and she invited them in to interview Washington. They wrote of the opulence and decor of her house, continuing the fascination with her wealth. After Washington departed, Walker was able to get him to agree to let her visit him at Tuskegee and spend a few days with him and his students.

When she arrived on the Tuskegee campus in February 1914, he greeted her smilingly. Her displays of wealth seemed to have worked on Washington, who had finally warmed to her when he came to believe she was a possible donor. He personally took her around the campus and had her address a group of students. Later he invited her back to his office. There he asked her to donate money to the Tuskegee Institute to support scholarships at the college. Madam agreed on a large donation in his office.

After she returned home, she sent a small donation

and wrote apologetically, "Next year I hope to be able to help you in a larger way." Washington, believing that she was holding out, wrote her a few months later, asking for another donation for scholarships for three students. Madam wrote back, "I am unlike your white friends who have waited until they were rich and then help," she admitted, conceding that she was not as liquid as her luxurious lifestyle suggested. "I have been mistaken for a rich woman, which has caused scores of demands for my help," she added. Despite feeling somewhat duped by her, Washington appreciated her for giving what she could. At the National Negro Business League conference, he invited her to speak and encouraged her to attend in future years.

In the months after that exchange, Booker T. Washington's health deteriorated rapidly due to severe hypertension. In 1915, he was ordered to take bed rest but refused and continued to work and travel. In November 1915, he collapsed from a stroke in New York while on a speaking tour. Doctors in New York told him he would not survive, and Washington asked to be sent home to Alabama. "I was born in the South, have lived all my life in the South, and expect to die and be buried in the South," he said. Washington was trained home to Tuskegee, where he died on November 14, 1915. The family of Robert Reed Church, Madam C. J. Walker, and Annie Malone all sent condolences to Tuskegee and mourned the death of a titan.

17

The Trials of Hannah Elias

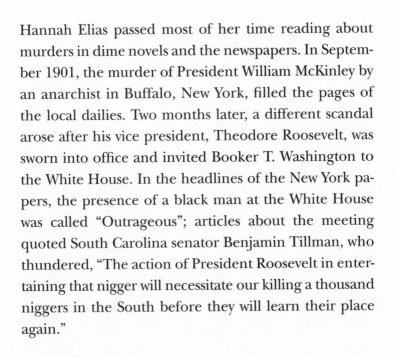

Hannah Elias passed most of her time reading about murders in dime novels and the newspapers. In September 1901, the murder of President William McKinley by an anarchist in Buffalo, New York, filled the pages of the local dailies. Two months later, a different scandal arose after his vice president, Theodore Roosevelt, was sworn into office and invited Booker T. Washington to the White House. In the headlines of the New York papers, the presence of a black man at the White House was called "Outrageous"; articles about the meeting quoted South Carolina senator Benjamin Tillman, who thundered, "The action of President Roosevelt in entertaining that nigger will necessitate our killing a thousand niggers in the South before they will learn their place again."

The same year Hannah became pregnant, and John Platt was presumed to be the father. The following spring, she delivered a baby girl at her home and named her Gwendolyn Elias. On the baby's birth certificate, she listed the child's race as white.

By recording Gwendolyn as white, Elias made manifest her hope that her daughter could achieve what Elias was unable to do herself: pass for white. Elias's life, even as a woman of means, was bounded by race. In her view, the only way to escape the limitations that came from being rich and black was to escape being black altogether.

Several weeks after her birth, the baby became sick and died. Elias consumed herself in making funeral plans, arranging for an elaborate marble mausoleum to be constructed at her daughter's grave site. The work totaled $15,000 ($422,560), and Platt paid the bill. He, however, did not attend the funeral. Having no other friends, Elias paid her staff to attend her daughter's burial. On the death certificate, Elias listed the child's race as black. As she was dead, there was no point continuing to pretend she was white.

ON FRIDAY, NOVEMBER 13, 1903, CORNELIUS WILLIAMS STOOD looking into the mirror of a public restroom in Manhattan, combed his hair, slicked it with pomade, trimmed his mustache with a straight razor, adjusted his gray three-piece suit, and placed a matching bowler hat atop his head. He then packed the razor, a gold-plated watch, and a revolver into his pockets. His mind was made up: today was the day he was going to find Hannah Elias and take revenge upon her.

Elias had evicted him from her boardinghouse eight years before, and since then, according to those who knew him, Williams had gone mad. He still carried a grudge against her, and after being evicted from another house a month prior, he had resolved to track her down. When he found her, he was determined to "cut her tongue out."

However, he hadn't been able to locate Elias. No one at the church or the black social or eating establishments had seen her in years. Williams decided to extract her whereabouts from Platt, whom he knew by his pseudonym, "Mr. Green," and with whom he had once had a run-in at Elias's boardinghouse.

Several days earlier, Williams had found a man named Andrew Green in the city directory and had gone to the address of the office listed for him. Leering through a window at Green's office building, Williams saw an elderly white man with a beard and white hair and was sure he had his man. The man he saw, though, was not Platt, it was the New York city planner, Andrew H. Green.

On the morning of November 13, Williams went to the address listed as Green's residence on Park Avenue and waited for him to show up. Green lived in a town house with a covered staircase leading up to a front door of carved stone. When he arrived home at around noon, he found Williams waiting for him on the stairs.

As soon as he walked up, Williams began demanding to know Elias's whereabouts. "Who are you anyway? I don't know you! Get away from me!" Green shouted at Williams. Williams responded by taking his revolver from his hip pocket and shooting him three times, once in the head, once in the abdomen, and once more in the groin.

Williams took off after the shooting but ran back to the stoop in a panic when neighbors spotted him and shouted for him to stop. Standing over Green's lifeless body, Williams gesticulated and yelled obscenities. "You forced me to do it!" he was overheard yelling.

After a few minutes, a police carriage pulled up, and officers jumped out. Williams told the officer calmly, "I am the man who did the shooting," and pointed to a revolver in his hip pocket. The officer took the gun from him and placed him under arrest. "Officer, this is the man I wanted to shoot and I done it. I don't want to shoot anybody else, and you need not be afraid," he said as the officer wrestled him onto the police wagon.

They took Williams to the 34th Street police station for questioning. There he was interrogated by Captain Day. He told Day that he had killed Green because he was the lover of a woman who had slandered him. Day asked if Williams had ever been in a mental institution. "I have been called foolish sometimes but never insane. I am not insane," Williams replied, fidgeting with his mustache as his eyes darted up and down. He then posed for a mug shot in his chair. He puffed out his chest and sat up straight as the flashbulb went off.

That night, Williams slept soundly in a cell. In the morning, he sent out for a hearty breakfast. As he ate, police formed a committee to determine his sanity and assigned detectives to find and question Hannah Elias.

On Saturday, November 14, 1903, the front pages of newspapers across the country carried banner headlines with the news of the murder of New York's city planner by a "crazed Negro" seeking revenge against Green's black mistress.

Throughout New York, flags were lowered to half-mast for the man who had unified the five boroughs into one city and overseen the construction of the Metropolitan Museum of Art, the American Museum of Natural History, the Bronx Zoo, the New York Public Library, and Central Park. Even as they mourned, though, New Yorkers were shocked that Green had been shot over a black woman. On the steps of Green's house, still stained with blood, his nephew addressed a group of reporters, attempting to quell the rumors of an interracial liaison. "The story that this negro tells is a perfect humbug and a fiction from A to Z," he told the scrum of reporters.

Inspector George W. McClusky was tasked with finding the woman Williams had spoken of. He discovered Hannah Elias residing in a mansion at 236 Central Park West. He went to her house that morning and was let in by her staff, who led him to Elias sprawled on a sofa in her best Cleopatra pose. She told McClusky that

Williams's statement was "a tissue of lies." She then admitted that Williams had lived in her lodging house in 1895, but swore she had never heard from him since he had left. She denied knowing or meeting Green but told McClusky that Green resembled a man she was having an affair with, John R. Platt.

That same evening, McClusky visited Platt at his house to confirm Elias's story. Platt's son-in-law, W. J. Cassard, was at home with Platt and insisted on being present for his questioning. Platt told McClusky that Elias's story was true but asked that his affair with her be kept confidential. McClusky agreed. However, Platt's secret affair had now been revealed to his family.

Williams was deemed insane a week after the murder and committed to an asylum. McClusky, true to his word, kept Platt's affair from reaching the papers. Platt's relatives were another matter; Cassard shared the secret with the rest of Platt's family, who became outraged when they found out how much of his fortune, which they stood to inherit, had been lavished on his black mistress.

ON TUESDAY, MAY 30, 1904, JOHN R. PLATT, UNDER PRESSURE FROM his family, filed a lawsuit against Hannah Bessie Elias in the amount of $685,385 ($18.5 million) in New York Superior Court. In the suit, which his lawyers from the firm of Warren, Warren & O'Beirne published in the local papers, he alleged that Elias had extorted money from him over the previous eight years. The lawsuit also requested that all her accounts, which included holdings in twenty-six savings institutions, thirty-four trust companies, and sixty-nine banks, be frozen. It also requested that she be prevented from selling any of the twelve properties she owned, including her boardinghouse in Midtown, her Central Park West mansion, or her rental properties in upper Manhattan.

It had taken months of convincing by Platt's younger brother, Isaac S. Platt, and W. J. Cassard, to get Platt to sign off on the lawsuit. "They convinced me that the woman was determined to ruin not only my reputation in the end, but in the meantime to squeeze all the money possible out of me," he explained. The one concession he demanded from his relatives was that Elias not be arrested.

When Elias heard the news, she panicked. She flew into a fit and began barking orders at her servants to run to the banks where she had holdings and drain her accounts. When they returned later in the day, they told her that they had not been able to get all the money. Collectively they had come up with $156,000 ($4.2 million) in cash. Elias put the money into a sack, gave it to her doorman, Patrick W. Dugan, and instructed him to put it into a safe at his house. After her cash had been hidden, she collapsed and was carried to bed by her servants.

That evening, crowds of angry protesters and onlookers began to gather outside her home, their jeers coming through the walls and windows. One of Elias's servants fetched a chain to reinforce the doors for fear the crowd might climb the gates and kick them in.

As Elias had long feared, the public revelation of a black woman being in possession of such wealth caused outrage. Though some blacks were known to own businesses or work in trade jobs, it was unfathomable that a black woman was living next to millionaires and was perhaps a millionaire herself. Moreover, she was not even a full generation out of slavery; she had been born in the free territory of Philadelphia in August 1865, four months before the ratification of the Thirteenth Amendment.

The day after the suit was announced, Platt's lawyers obtained a civil order for Elias's arrest. They told a judge at the Superior Court that they feared she might flee to Japan with her butler Kato. The judge granted the order, which was given to a New York City deputy sheriff along with the mandate for her arrest.

When the deputy arrived at her house, he had to push past the crowd to climb the stairs of her home and ring the doorbell. Kato greeted him. The butler apologetically told the deputy that he had to deny him entrance to the house because Elias was ill. The deputy sheriff began shouting at Kato, at which point Washington Brauns, an attorney hired by Elias, arrived at the house and interceded.

"There is no reason on earth for trying to arrest my client," he told the deputy sheriff, getting between him and Kato. "She hasn't any idea of trying to get away, and even if she had she is too ill to do so."

After arguing back and forth with Brauns, the deputy conceded that the civil order for an arrest did not allow him forcible entry into the home; Elias could be arrested only on a criminal complaint.

For a week after the lawsuit was filed, Elias stayed in her home. Platt's attorney remained frustrated that they were unable to serve her with the lawsuit or the order for civil arrest. The crowd outside her home was now in the hundreds, the number having grown so large that it blocked the sidewalk and street, bringing carriage traffic to a halt. As the gathering outside her home grew larger, the prospect of violence loomed. A few days earlier, Kato and two black errand boys she employed had been assaulted when trying to leave the house. They had been able to flee back into the home with only a few bruises before things got too out of hand. Afterward, a mounted police detail had been assigned to her block to keep the crowd under control and the streets clear. However, as reinforcements arrived, the crowd seemed to increase by the hour, with one detective putting the number of people gathered at ten thousand.

The Elias scandal had been in the papers for days with writing that NEGRESS EXTORTED NEARLY $1,000,000 and PLATT SAYS ELIAS OBTAINED NEARLY $700,000 THROUGH THREATS. The ordeal seemed to spark racial outrage and inflame the economic tensions already simmering in the city. Protesting at Elias's house became so popular in the city that men and women were known to pack lunches and bring their children to stand outside her house to hurl profanity and trash at her windows.

At eight o'clock on June 7, two New York assistant district attorneys and a judge went to see Platt in his home, hoping to get him to sign a criminal complaint so that they could arrest Elias. Platt held out until ten o'clock, finally giving in to the persuasions of the judge, the attorneys, and his family. After they had received Platt's signature, the judge issued a warrant for Elias's arrest on the spot.

At eleven that night, detectives attempted to kick down her front door. The door resisted their boots, and one of the detectives sent a deputy to try to find an ax. Before he could return, someone from the crowd offered a heavy metal pipe, which a detective then used to batter the door until it gave in.

The detectives rushed inside the house to find it in complete darkness. Kato emerged from the shadows and politely greeted the detectives. "I will take you to her," he said, pointing toward a winding stairwell. Elias was sitting up in bed, still in her nightclothes. "We would have come to the door but it being such a late hour we weren't sure what to do," she explained. She told the officers she was prepared to come with them but needed a few minutes to dress.

As she exited the house with the officers, Elias wore a dark dress, a wig of straight black hair pinned into a bun, and a black veil attached to her hat. As she walked to the police carriage, the crowd became raucous, hurling bottles and rocks in her direction. She pressed her face into the arm of one of the detectives to shield herself from the debris.

When she arrived at the Tombs, as the City Prison was commonly known, she could hear screaming outside the carriage and objects breaking against its roof. Flanked by a group of officers, she ducked through another mob into the Tombs, where she was processed and booked just after 2 a.m. on June 8, 1904. From her cell, her screams and sobs could be heard echoing throughout the station.

Two days later, Hannah Elias was to be arraigned on charges of extortion in the New York Criminal Court building. The night before, she had stayed up all evening in her cell staring at a threatening letter she had received from the Duquesne Club in Pittsburgh, a social club composed of white male industrialists. She spent hours studying the words scrawled on the paper.

It was clear that the scandal of a wealthy black woman alleged to be an extortionist had drawn attention. Elias lived in a mansion off of Central Park outfitted with butlers, maids, and personal chefs from Japan, China, France, and Africa. She owned three properties in New York City in addition to her main home; she had a chauffeur and carriage, diamonds, pearls, and furs; she had over $100,000 ($2.7 million) in cash and rented a summer home in Long Branch, New Jersey. A rich black woman confounded ideas about blacks and poverty, while the accusation of blackmail against Platt gave support to stereotypes about blacks and criminality. Her story was being covered by newspapers across the country as readers followed along waiting to see what the conclusion would be.

At her arraignment, the crowd in the courtroom grew so large that the doors could barely be shut. Police barricaded the entrances to the courthouse to prevent the thousands gathered outside from forcing their way in.

Elias sat at the defense table with her lawyer, Washington Brauns, waiting for the proceedings to start. Across the courtroom was the prosecutor, Assistant District Attorney William Rand, who had the look of a man who was assured the outcome would be in his favor. The first witness Rand called that day was John R. Platt. As Platt climbed onto the witness stand, Elias leveled her gaze at him. When Platt shifted in his seat, Elias adjusted her position to fix her stare upon him again.

"How old are you?" the prosecutor began.

"I'm eighty-three years old. I was born in 1820," Platt replied.

"What is your occupation?"

"I have no occupation. I was a plate-glass manufacturer, but retired years ago," Platt answered.

"Do you know the defendant Hannah Elias, and if so, how long have you known her?"

"I know her, but I don't know just when I met her; it was a long time ago when the volunteer firemen came here from San Francisco."

"You supported her during the last ten years," District Attorney Rand posed, at which point Elias locked eyes with Platt.

"I don't know," Platt said, searching for the right answer. "I have given her large sums of money."

"Your relations with her have been more than a friend, have they not?"

"Yes." Platt seemed bothered by the question.

"Did you give her large sums of money for the last ten years running into the hundreds of thousands of dollars?"

"I don't know," Platt said. His answer brought a look of displeasure to Rand's face.

"Do you remember bringing action in the Supreme Court to recover $685,000?"

"I don't know," Platt muttered.

"Do you remember any of the suit at all?" Rand asked.

"I don't know," Platt repeated.

"Do you remember signing a warrant charging her with blackmail?"

"I think I did."

"Do you know what day of the week it is?" Rand asked, growing impatient.

"I think so."

"Do you know what day of the month it is?"

"I don't remember," Platt replied, his answer seeming to throw the prosecutor into a fit of anger.

"Do you remember swearing to certain facts in this case the other night in your home?" Rand pounded the table in front of him.

"Go easy on the witness!" the judge interjected. Rand posed several dozen more questions, to which Platt replied, "I don't know" or "I don't remember," until the prosecutor finally gave up. Elias's attorney declined to cross-examine Platt. A former attorney of Elias's was called, testifying that he had known of Platt and Elias's affair but had no knowledge of where she got her money. Both of his witnesses having fallen flat, Rand told the judge he had no other evidence to present.

Magistrate Ommen spoke up. "I wish to place myself right. The district attorney has not made out the case as he did at the conference at Mr. Platt's house," he said, seemingly apologetic. After scolding the district attorney for his presentation of the case, he looked at Rand and uttered what sounded like a question but seemed to be an order. "Do I understand the district attorney requests the dismissal of the charge against the woman?"

"You can put it that the district attorney's office recommends that such a course be pursued," Rand conceded.

After the case was dismissed and the court adjourned, Platt exited the courtroom first, leaving through the front door, leaning on his cane. Jeers of "nigger lover" and a cascade of bottles greeted him. Police escorted Elias and her lawyer to a back exit, where a carriage awaited. They returned to her mansion, taking back streets to avoid the crowds. Kato was waiting when they pulled up. Elias and Brauns ran up the stairs and shared an embrace with him.

Later that evening, Elias invited a rare guest into her home, a reporter from the *New York Times*. Seated in the parlor of her home, she gave her first public statement.

"I don't blame the poor old man at all," she told the reporter. "I know he was forced to bring the suit against me, and he had no choice in the matter of sending out the warrant for my arrest. He never wanted to make trouble for me himself. I am sure of it. I've known all along I would be vindicated as soon as I got a hearing. I never did anything wrong taking the money which he gave me. It's all nonsense to talk of me having blackmailed him, as he plainly showed himself this afternoon when he refused to say that I extorted money from him by threats."

Elias, who had dealt with the angry crowds outside her home for weeks, seemed to reach for conciliation in her final words: "I have all my life made white people my friends and never had much to do with my own race."

The crowds outside her home shrank each day after the trial until one day, after a few weeks, they were gone altogether. Looking out her window, Elias could see an empty strip of pavement in front of her home and again see the green of the park. She took it as an auspicious sign and hoped that the worst of her misfortunes were over.

18

Black Millionaire Legacy

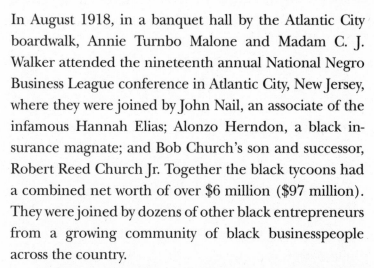

In August 1918, in a banquet hall by the Atlantic City boardwalk, Annie Turnbo Malone and Madam C. J. Walker attended the nineteenth annual National Negro Business League conference in Atlantic City, New Jersey, where they were joined by John Nail, an associate of the infamous Hannah Elias; Alonzo Herndon, a black insurance magnate; and Bob Church's son and successor, Robert Reed Church Jr. Together the black tycoons had a combined net worth of over $6 million ($97 million). They were joined by dozens of other black entrepreneurs from a growing community of black businesspeople across the country.

James Carrol Napier, the late Booker T. Washington's successor as the president of the National Negro Business League, presided over the festivities. Napier had beige skin and wispy white hair. He dressed in three-piece suits with gold pocket watch chains and spoke with a strong Nashville southern drawl. The league discussed the grocery business in black communities as well as support for black farms. They discussed the life insurance business and investing in real estate.

Chief on the minds of the members of the league as they sat together in the banquet hall was World War I. John Nail, New York's top real estate developer, and a returned World War veteran, listened intently as Napier waxed on about how it was paramount for the efforts of African American soldiers in the war to be publicized. Then the discussion turned to business. Dr. R. R. Moton, an administrator at the Tuskegee Institute, took the floor to submit a plan for how black businesses could take advantage of the "more favorable economic conditions" presented to them by the war.

Later, the group moved to congratulate Annie Malone on the completion of Poro College in St. Louis, and Madam was briefly given the floor to advocate for a resolution to praise George W. Breckenridge, a white newspaper publisher who had pledged $100,000 ($1.6 million) to combat lynchers.

After Atlantic City, Madam C. J. Walker continued her rise to celebrity. In 1918, the Madam C. J. Walker Manufacturing Company brought in $275,937.88 ($4.4 million) in revenue, half of which was profit; it had made about $150,000 the previous year. "I have no doubt that you can easily make half a million in 1919," her manager, Freeman Ransom, wrote Madam just after New Year's of 1919. The previous year, he had told Madam that her expenditures dwarfed her income by almost $200,000 ($3.2 million), as she had spent $329,016.85 ($5.3 million) building a mansion, Villa Lewaro, in upstate Irvington, New York. "This makes an apparent deficit, which is of course offset by loans etc." Ransom informed Madam that she had $5,228.27 ($84,880.54) in the bank at the time of the writing. However, the projections for 1919 were looking good, so her coffers would soon be full again.

That year, the Walker Company took in $12,000 ($169,555) of revenue in the month of January. That month, Madam went to Tiffany & Co. at 37th Street and 5th Avenue and bought a 3.38-carat solitaire diamond set in platinum surrounded by sixty-six tiny diamonds and matching earrings. The purchase nearly ate up her entire profit for the month. Madam spoiled herself, but she had failed to look after her health. She had developed hypertension and had lived with the ailment for years, but the strain of her frequent travels and the stress of running her company made it difficult to keep her symptoms at bay.

Four months later, in May 1919, just after moving into her upstate mansion, Madam collapsed in her parlor. She died of kidney failure shortly thereafter. At the time of her death she had a net worth of just over half a million dollars.

After her death, Freeman Ransom decided to publicize that she had been a millionaire. He realized that the future of the Walker Company and estate depended on her memory. He had long realized that women bought

Walker products because they wanted to be like Madam, a slave's daughter who had risen to fame and fortune.

Ransom created press releases for black newspapers that implied that Madam had been a millionaire. The tactic worked, and soon the legend began to be repeated as fact. Under Ransom's direction the company brought in a million dollars in a two-year span from 1919 to 1920, perhaps its most competitive year with Poro, which did more than $3 million ($36.6 million) of business in the same period. The surge was short-lived as the revenue fell in the 1920s before the Great Depression in 1929 dealt a near-death blow to the company. By 1931, Madam's mansion, Villa Lewaro, was on the market, her properties in Indianapolis rented out. The Walker Company was struggling to stay afloat, and her daughter, A'Lelia Walker, was pawning her jewelry for money. In August 1931, A'Lelia died of a brain hemorrhage.

Like her late rival, Annie became overly concerned with showing off her wealth. In 1920, she made a splash when she bought a Rolls-Royce. That year she made more than $4 million ($48.8 million) and paid the second-highest income tax in the state of Missouri. In 1924, she gave $25,000 ($357,410) to the Indianapolis YMCA, where Madam had been able to make a splash with a $1,000 ($24,633) donation. Outside of the St. Louis press, the gift was largely unreported. Annie grew frustrated by the lack of recognition. She berated her employees, and she and her husband fought loudly in public.

In 1926, Aaron filed for divorce and sought half of

Annie's empire. In the end, after a costly court battle, she was forced to give Aaron $200,000 ($2.7 million). It was the beginning of financial troubles as she spent the next decade trying to spend her way into relevance, giving six-figure donations to causes only to achieve minimal press coverage. Her out-of-control spending forced her to default on her taxes, and by 1943, she owed $100,000 ($906,888) to the IRS and a lien was placed on her assets.

In her later years Annie continued to struggle over money, and the Poro Company faded. On May 10, 1957, she died at age eighty-seven. In some of the publications that carried the news of her death she was eulogized as Madam C. J. Walker's mentor.

19

End of the Promise

Gurley's reputation in Greenwood was boosted by his beating of the three white men who harassed his wife. For a moment it seemed that the richest black man in Greenwood was putting aside his ambition and pragmatism and becoming a man of the people.

It didn't last. In 1918, O. W. Gurley was charged with bribery by two women in Greenwood. According to the complaint, Gurley took two rings from the two black women "to keep them out of jail." Gurley, who was a Tulsa sheriff's deputy and charged with policing Greenwood, was rumored to have regularly demanded bribes from people accused of crimes in Greenwood in exchange for not arresting them. Gurley escaped jail and kept his sheriff's deputy badge, but rumors of corruption dented his reputation.

In 1919, as the black newspapers carried news of Madam C. J. Walker's death, three black men were arrested in Tulsa on the suspicion of shooting a white ironworker. The men were transported to the Tulsa County jail, just across the train tracks from Greenwood in the white section of Tulsa, and put into a cell together.

Word traveled through the grapevine back to Tulsa that a white mob had plans to take the men from the cell that night and lynch them. Within hours a posse of black men was organized. More than two dozen black men carrying revolvers and rifles marched across the train tracks to the jail and barged in. They demanded to see the prisoners and got into a shouting match with the police. As the confrontation escalated, men on both sides began to move their fingers toward the triggers of their guns.

As the tension reached a breaking point, Gurley sauntered through the door. His hair was now gray and he wore glasses with thick circular lenses. He was a rich man and wore an expensive suit on his broad frame with a sheriff's star pinned to his breast and a pistol at his side. He walked up to the police chief, and the two walked away conversing in whispers. A few moments later a deal had been brokered: Gurley was given assurances that the men wouldn't be harmed, and the police would allow the group from Greenwood to check on the prisoners if they left immediately thereafter. A delegation of the men from the group escorted by an officer went back to check on the men in the cell. A few minutes later they came back, reporting that the prisoners were being treated well, and the men went back to Greenwood. The aftermath would send chills through white Tulsa. The independence and strength of Greenwood had been reluctantly tolerated as long as Gurley could keep the blacks under control, but this "armed invasion," as it was later called, set off alarms. The negroes were getting out of their place.

A few months later, a white man was accused of assaulting a black woman on a trolley in downtown Tulsa. Gurley obtained a warrant for the man but was forbidden from arresting him. Tulsa's sheriff, Willard McCullough, reportedly ripped the warrant from Gurley's hands, stating he "would never allow a black man to serve a warrant on a white man in Tulsa." In response, Gurley resigned as a sheriff's deputy and handed McCullough his badge.

BY 1921, GURLEY WAS THE RICHEST AND MOST POWERFUL MAN IN Greenwood. He was landlord to almost half the town's residents and shopkeepers, collecting $5,000 ($68,318) a month in rents. With more than a hundred properties in Greenwood, he was worth between $500,000 and $1 million (between $6.8 million and $13.6 million). His net worth could only be guessed at in Greenwood, as Gurley kept his own money across the tracks in the white banks in downtown Tulsa. His hotel, valued at least $99,000 ($1.35 million), was one of the busiest in the district.

J. B. Stradford, Greenwood's other founding father, was growing more popular. In 1918, he helped organize an armed group to turn back a lynch mob in nearby Bristow, Oklahoma. In Greenwood, Stradford's more militant approach to civil rights became increasingly popular. In 1920, with the help of A. J. Smitherman, he brought W. E. B. Du Bois to Greenwood. Gurley didn't protest; in fact, he put him up in his hotel. Du Bois gave several lectures to the residents, focusing on the need for blacks to become economically self-reliant and push back against lynching. In a fiery speech in a theater, he looked out onto the faces of hundreds of Tulsa blacks and spoke romantically about the burgeoning artistic renaissance in Harlem, New York; advocated for African Americans to organize for their rights; and urged the people of Greenwood to protect their own people from lynching.

ON A RAINY MEMORIAL DAY IN 1921, DICK ROWLAND ENTERED THE Drexel Building in Tulsa through two glass doors to use the only colored bathroom on the block, which was at the top of the building. Rowland was a nineteen-year-old high school dropout who worked shining shoes at a stand outside the office building. He was tall, confident, and outgoing. In Greenwood, where he had grown up and still resided, he was known for being ostentatious, showing his billfold, and wearing an earring with his nickname, "Diamond Dick," but was thought by most to be harmless. He walked through the lobby and entered the elevator. On board was the elevator operator, a seventeen-year-old white girl named Sarah Page. The door closed for a moment, and then a scream came out. When the doors opened again, Sarah ran away. A white clerk who had heard her scream called the police. When the police arrived, they didn't make much of the incident. They questioned Rowland, sent him home, and quietly began to ask around about the incident. "We did not attach sufficient importance to the event," one police captain remembered. It all just seemed like a misunderstanding.

The next day newspaper boys greeted people in the streets, pushing papers with the headline NAB NEGRO FOR ATTACKING GIRL IN ELEVATOR. "Negro assaults white girl!" they cried. The evidence that anything had happened was flimsy, but stories of black-on-white sexual assault always made for lucrative headlines and strong newspaper sales. The details of the story were mostly fabricated; nevertheless, they incited calls for Rowland to be locked up or worse. Later that day, the same officers who had let Rowland go went to his house, took him away, and put him into a cell in the courthouse.

Once Rowland was in jail, talk of lynching him spread among white men in Tulsa. Calls began to come into the police chief about the organizing of lynch mobs. The next day, the *Tulsa Tribune* ran an editorial encouraging lynching titled TO LYNCH A NEGRO TONIGHT.

LATE THAT AFTERNOON, O. W. GURLEY ARRIVED AT THE COURThouse to see the police chief. He, too, had heard that a lynch mob was being gathered for Rowland. "Gurley, there won't be any lynching, as long as I'm sheriff," he assured Gurley. "If you keep your folks away from here, there won't be any trouble." Gurley accepted his assurance and headed back to Greenwood to try to keep things under control.

The police hoped that if they could prevent a racial standoff, bloodshed could be avoided. Early in the evening, the police chief's phone rang. A voice said, "We are going to lynch that negro tonight, that black devil that assaulted that white girl." Then the line went dead. A few hours later, a crowd gathered on the courthouse steps with men demanding that Dick Rowland be brought out. "You might as well go home because no one is going to get the negro," the police chief told the mob leaders.

Inside, Sarah Page was being questioned by police officers. She said the incident might have been a mistake and she equivocated about pressing charges. Nonetheless, the white mob outside grew angrier and angrier even as the sexual assault accusation was falling apart. Rowland's cell was on the top floor of the courthouse, accessible only by an elevator. The chief ordered five deputies to disable the elevator and stand guard in front of its door. Nobody would be lynching him tonight.

When Gurley returned from the courthouse he found men in Greenwood in a state of agitation over fears that Rowland would be lynched. Many younger men were gathering ammunition and weapons and planning to go to the courthouse to protect Rowland. Gurley spoke to a group of them in the street outside his hotel. He told them that he had just spoken with the authorities and that the police would protect Rowland. "You're a damn liar!" a man named Anderson shouted at Gurley. "They're going to take this nigger out!" "Fellow, you ought to be put in jail right now," Gurley snapped back at Anderson. The man pulled his pistol from his hip and aimed it at Gurley, who was sure he was about to be shot. An older lawyer named Spears jumped in between them and talked Anderson into putting the gun away.

Down the street, a lawyer named B. C. Franklin heard the fracas and rushed from his rooming house into the street. He found two World War I veterans, one black and one white, exciting the crowd with talk of war. "We need to bomb one of the buildings!" they shouted. Franklin, a hypnotic orator, told the crowd that such action would lead to the destruction of Greenwood and possibly the deaths of everyone there. After his speech, the crowd dispersed.

Despite the best efforts of Gurley and Greenwood's elders, a group of seventy-five lightly armed men left Greenwood and went to the courthouse at 7:30 that night. Police chief Willard McCullough dispatched a deputy to deal with them when they arrived. "Boy, where are you going?" the deputy asked. "We're coming to see about that lynching," one of the Greenwood men said. The deputy replied, "Now, this boy is upstairs and the cage is locked upstairs, and there is no way anyone can get him. Go back." The group left without incident, walking north across the train tracks to Greenwood.

A little over an hour later, as Greenwood's elders went back to their homes, young men and women gathered in pool halls, bars, and theaters. Among them, a wild rumor somehow spread that Rowland had been taken from the jail and lynched. By 9:30, a group of men with guns drove down to the courthouse. As they arrived, the barrels of their rifles and pistols gleamed under the streetlights. The police chief came out to deal with them. "Now you men listen to me!" he shouted. "Go home before a lot of people get hurt. You have no business coming up here parading around guns like that. If you are law-abiding people, you will go home before the real trouble starts." "We will go home when we get that Negro boy you want to lynch!" one of the men shouted back, as others cheered him. "We ain't going nowhere," they chorused. "No one is going to be lynched here," the police chief told them. "There is not going to be a charge against the young man. The white girl had admitted that he did not harm her. She said she was nervous and scared, so she screamed when he grabbed her. That is all there is to this case. She is a very nervous person, but she said she is not going to press charges as no harm was done. So go home now. I give you my word the Negro will be released in the morning." "If there's no charge, why don't you turn him over to us now?" a man asked. "That is not possible," the sheriff answered. "Why not?" another asked. "Because he's telling a damn lie!" another shouted. "If we leave him here, he's a goner. They'll hang him like Judgment Day." The sheriff remained calm. "Listen to me," he said. "Nobody is going to hang anybody from this jail, but I can't turn him over to you tonight. Only a judge can release somebody who's been charged with a crime." He then added, "We can't give in to lawlessness, so go home before trouble starts." The men mumbled among themselves, then turned and went home to Greenwood. A large group of them retreated to the bars and began drinking. Shortly after they left, a group of armed white men showed up. They stationed themselves around the courthouse, readying themselves to fight if another group of armed black men returned.

Late in the evening, after the bars and theaters closed for the night, a group of the men who had gone to the courthouse earlier made their way back, still armed and now drunk. They flashed their guns as they approached and again confronted the sheriff on the courthouse steps. "Parading around with those guns is against the law," he told them as the white mob watched. "Violence is easy to start but hard to stop." He pointed to the top floor of the courthouse, where snipers were positioned with rifles. "Look up at those windows. See those gun barrels pointed at you. They will cut you down before the first person reaches the courthouse. Now go home before a lot of people get shot."

As he was speaking, a white man approached the steps.

"Nigger, what are you going to do with that pistol?"

"I'm going to use it if I need to."

"No, you give it to me."

"Like hell I will."

The two men then began to struggle over the gun. A shot was discharged into the air as they fought. Then all hell broke loose.

A hail of bullets came from the white mob, hitting several of the blacks on the steps. Those who could moved into alleys and started to run toward Greenwood. Men in cars with gun barrels protruding from the windows mowed down people who tried to escape, as others were picked off by gunfire from the mob of white men gathered at the foot of the courthouse.

As the men raced back into Greenwood, the rioters followed them, shooting up buildings. The initial gunfire was followed by explosions as groups of armed white men moved from the courthouse steps into Greenwood. The men fired guns into buildings and homes and threw bombs through windows.

Gurley was lying awake in bed with his wife, Emma, in their apartment on the top floor of the Gurley hotel when the fighting started. He could smell smoke and hear the gunfire in the distance. When the sun came up he looked out his window to see smoke and flames. The violence had been followed by waves of looters who burned blacks out of their homes and looted stores, taking some blacks as hostages and killing others in the streets. Gurley ran downstairs and outside into the street and the smoke-filled air. He heard gunshots and cracking fire. Greenwood was burning.

Through the smoke, he saw six white men down the street holding shotguns, rifles, jugs of gasoline, and torches. One of the men walked up on Gurley and motioned toward his hotel. "You better get out of that hotel because we're gonna burn all this goddam stuff," he said. "You better get all your guests out." The men left Gurley and went down the street, door to door, telling people to evacuate before they started burning.

Gurley ran back inside and found Emma sitting in a rocking chair near the window of the bedroom looking outside and shaking in fright. "We need to go, Emma. Their fire is going to get us," he told her. "It's going to get everyone."

"But where will we go if the fire is everywhere?" Emma said.

"I don't know," Gurley replied.

The Gurleys decided to try to run south across the train tracks to white Tulsa. The people knew Gurley there. He'd been the reasonable one who had tried to keep the young men of Greenwood in line. Surely they'd spare him. Surely someone would give him shelter. When they got outside, two white men with guns started shooting at the couple. Emma fell to the ground. "Don't worry about me. You need to run," she told Gurley. Gurley took off without saying good-bye or looking back.

As Gurley ran, he saw the National Guard and mobs of white men pouring into Greenwood. He was grabbed by some members of the guard, who were removing blacks from Greenwood and "quarantining" them at a baseball park just across the tracks.

⌁

AT THE PARK, GURLEY WAS ISOLATED. THE CONSTITUENTS OF THE district he built stared at him without speaking. They blamed him. His racial conciliation. His self-interest. "My lord, it's Gurley!" OW turned to see Emma up in the stadium's bleachers. She ran down to Gurley and they embraced.

OW had lost the faith of his people, he had lost his dream, and he would eventually lose more than $250,000 ($3.4 million) in the riots, but at that moment, he was glad he hadn't lost Emma, too.

After the riots, he tried to sell his ruined lands to the local railroad company for $25,000 ($340,000), but the deal fell through.

In the months afterward, he moved to a four-bedroom house in South Los Angeles and opened a hotel. A rumor spread that he was dead, that he had been lynched during the violence. Gurley was not dead, but his dream was. In the end, he sold his land to other African Americans in Greenwood who ultimately stayed there and began to rebuild.

In 1926, W. E. B. Du Bois visited Greenwood. The riot's damage had been repaired, and new buildings had risen. Looking on the resilient black faces of the Promised Land, he wrote, "Black Tulsa is a happy city.

It has new clothes. It is young and gay and strong. Five little years ago, fire and blood and robbery leveled it to the ground. Scars are there, but the city is impudent and noisy. It believes in itself. Thank God for the grit of Black Tulsa."

20

Paris by Way of Harlem

In July 1906, after the trial of Hannah Elias, two apartment buildings on West 135th Street in Harlem were purchased by an anonymous buyer through the Afro-American Realty Company for $100,000 ($2.7 million). A few days later, notes were slipped under the doors of the white families in the buildings. The notes told them to vacate their homes within twenty-four hours and that in the future the dwellings would only be rented to "respectable colored families."

After the tenants got their eviction notices, the papers howled, WHITE TENANTS EVICTED BY HANNAH ELIAS. An article published in the *New York Evening World* read, "Hannah Elias the negress that got $685,000 from John R. Platt has jarred a goodly part of Harlem by ordering all the white tenants out of two big flat buildings." The article concluded that her move was part of a larger plot. "This indicates that the wealthy colored woman will make a colored settlement out of one of the choicest neighborhoods above 125th street."

Elias denied having any part in the building purchases or the evictions, but she had indeed begun investing in Harlem with a handful of other powerful African Americans. The upper Manhattan neighborhood was nearly all white, but changes were afoot. It stretched from the top of Central Park at 110th Street fifty blocks north to 160th Street, backing up to the deep woods that surrounded Fort Washington. The area was dotted with farms, Victorian mansions, wood-frame homes with lawns, new brownstones, and empty lots on a grid of tree-lined streets. Andrew Green, the New York City planner whose murder Elias had indirectly been involved in, had facilitated the development of two elevated trains that connected Harlem to lower Manhattan. When the commuter rails had opened at the turn of the century, they had set off waves of migration to Harlem. The first migrants were white Manhattanites, Eastern European and Italian immigrants. They were followed a few years later by middle-class African Americans. Blacks began moving to Harlem with the help of an African American real estate developer named Philip A. Payton Jr., and his company, the Afro-American Realty Company. The first African American migrants to Harlem came from Greenwich Village in Manhattan and Brooklyn and met resistance from whites as soon as they arrived. "Their presence is undesirable among us [in Harlem]," an entry in the *New York Indicator*, a Manhattan real estate journal, stated, adding that blacks should be "seg-regated into some colony in the outskirts of the city, where their transportation and other problems will not inflict injustice and disgust on other worthy citizens." As the Afro-American Realty Company helped blacks move into lower Harlem, the neighborhood's white citizens organized to prevent blacks from moving deeper in. Led by John G. Tyler, a white separatist Harlemite and real estate developer, a slew of antiblack, anti-integration proponents quickly began to organize: the Save-Harlem Committee, Anglo-Saxon Realty, and the Harlem Property Owners' Association.

After blacks rapidly moved into lower Harlem after the opening of the train station at 125th Street in 1905, whites focused their efforts on preventing blacks from encroaching higher, drawing a line at 130th Street, which served as the border between integrated and nonintegrated Harlem. In 1909, white Harlemites suc-cessfully lobbied the New York Public Library on 135th Street to ban blacks from using the facilities. In 1912, a group of wealthy white industrialists, including the department store magnate Erduin van der Horst Koch, forced the eviction of black tenants on 131st and 132nd Streets and blocked a black movie theater from open-ing on Lenox Avenue near 130th Street. Although some elite African Americans such as Elias had luck early on buying property in "white Harlem" above 130th Street, as the white residents organized, others found it impos-sible to penetrate the upper portion of the neighbor-hood, which had wider streets and larger homes.

In 1911, John Nail, one of the top agents of the Afro-American Realty Company, left to form his own real estate business. In his new endeavor he had one very wealthy client of note: Hannah Elias. Nail was a handsome man with brown skin, a round face, and curly brown hair who wore bespoke suits and highly polished shoes. He came from a prestigious family and was the brother-in-law of the NAACP's James Weldon Johnson. He and Elias became friends after her trial. With his smarts and clients like Elias, Nail had a plan to begin to bypass the color line at 130th Street and become the biggest real estate agent in Harlem.

Nail had a secret weapon: his pastor, Reverend Hutchens C. Bishop. Bishop presided over St. Philips Episcopal Church, of which Nail and Elias were both members. With his olive-colored skin, blue eyes, straight nose, square jaw, and straight brown hair, which he slicked tightly back, Bishop could pass for a white man.

He was descended from freed blacks in Baltimore and considered his church a "high church," recruiting upper-class African Americans such as Elias and Nail to his flock. St. Philips Episcopal Church became famous among African Americans during the Civil War Draft Riots in 1863, when more than a hundred black New Yorkers were killed by mobs and the property of famous African Americans such as Jeremiah Hamilton and James McCune Smith was attacked. During the riots, thousands of blacks sheltered in St. Philip's, which had stone walls and thick wooden doors. In 1906, as his flock swelled to more than a thousand souls, Bishop decided to move to a larger church in Harlem. In 1906, Nail and Bishop sold his church building in Hell's Kitchen for $600,000 ($16.2 million) and purchased a new church on 135th Street in "white Harlem."

Bishop went by himself to purchase the church and put the building into his own name. Looking into the reverend's sparkling blue eyes, the sellers never imagined they were selling to a black man, let alone a large black church congregation. After purchasing the church, Bishop and Nail bought six more apartments in "white Harlem" using the same scheme. After Nail established his own company with Elias's financial backing, he deployed Bishop as a straw buyer, gobbling up dozens of properties.

Once they had acquired properties, Nail began renting and selling them to African Americans. His first customers were upper-class African Americans from the neighborhoods of Williamsburg and downtown Brooklyn, where he had grown up. Nail sold them lots for $1,000 to $3,000 to build homes on. After the Draft Riots, affluent African Americans, many of whose families and businesses had been attacked by mobs, had fled Manhattan for Brooklyn. Nail successfully recruited dozens of affluent black families back to Manhattan, promising them that Harlem would be a haven for blacks on the island. Later he bought and built apartment buildings and rented apartments to working-class African Americans, who were turned away by white landlords in other areas of New York. Between 1911 and 1914, he bought up more than $1.1 million ($27.6 million) worth of property in Harlem. With the help of Elias and Bishop, he helped break the color line at 130th Street and turn Harlem into a bustling black enclave.

AFTER THEIR AFFAIR AND RESULTING SCANDAL, ELIAS'S EX-LOVER John Platt stayed in New York City and moved to upper Manhattan, living with one of his daughters. "I've got to stay and face the music," he told friends and family members. He appealed the decision to dismiss his blackmail charge against Elias in court but lost. He remained estranged from her after taking her to court, but kept tabs of her activities in the papers. He read stories about her whenever they were published. In 1908, he died of a heart attack at the age of eighty-nine; he left nothing to Elias in his will. She knew better than to attend his funeral. Platt's estate was worth $10,000 ($270,000) at the time of his death. It seemed that the former millionaire had transferred the majority of his wealth to Elias during their affair.

In 1910, Elias left her mansion at Central Park West and moved to the penthouse of an apartment building she owned on 113th and Broadway with her butler Kato. In Harlem, she did not have to shutter her windows or hide her face behind a veil. For a time, she felt free. After a few years, the knocks on the door began. As the best-known wealthy black woman in New York, she was constantly hassled by people looking for charity and sheriff's deputies serving her with lawsuits. She was sued by her lawyers and contractors who said she owed them money for work they did for her. She bought a parakeet that she kept in a golden cage, which she screamed at when she was upset, and spent hours at a time berating and taking out her frustrations on Kato. In time she began to seclude herself in her penthouse the same way she had in her mansion.

IN 1914, AT THE BEGINNING OF WORLD WAR I, NAIL ENTERED THE US military as part of a cohort of African American men who hoped that blacks' participation in the armed services would help the cause of racial equality by demonstrating that blacks were patriots. Nail was part of a group of African American soldiers deployed to France during the war. When he returned to Harlem at the end of the war in 1918, his company continued to sell houses to African Americans and build apartments. Nail, like many other African American soldiers, was disappointed as he read about continued lynchings and voter suppression in black newspapers and the syndicated columns of Ida B. Wells. In 1921, as he was returning hundreds of thousands of dollars (millions today) to Hannah Elias in profits, the race riots in Greenwood hit the papers. On June 10, the *New York Age*, Harlem's paper of record, carried the headline on its front page: OKLAHOMA WHITES ATTEMPT TO DESTROY ENTIRE NEGRO SECTION—EXTRA—75 DEAD, BOTH RACES, MANY WOUNDED. In the months after the riots, a handful of African American survivors from Tulsa showed up in Harlem; Nail helped them get settled and found them apartments. Harlem became a destination for the black elite, with Madam C. J. Walker's family moving to the neighborhood in 1910 and Robert Reed Church's son Thomas Church moving there in 1919.

IN 1923, ELIAS DECIDED TO LEAVE THE UNITED STATES. SHE TOOK a car to New York pier and waited for a cruise liner that would carry her to Europe. She was accompanied by Kato, her butler and loyal companion. Elias planned to travel to France, where Nail had friends from World War I who had stayed in Europe after the war deployment. The black ex-soldiers stayed in Montmartre, a bohemia on a hilltop overlooking Paris where people from various backgrounds lived together.

When their ship arrived at New York Harbor, Elias and Kato boarded and sailed off across the Atlantic. Some people who knew her said she lived to old age in the South of France; others said she died in Paris a few years after arriving. One rumor said she had taken a million dollars with her; others cited the numerous lawsuits against her, insisting that she had been down to her last penny by the time she left. The one thing no one can disagree on is that she disappeared.

When the newspapers learned of her departure, they went to John Nail's office and inquired about his business associate's whereabouts. Nail told them nothing other than, "Hannah Elias has left." Elias had finally gotten what she wanted: no one could bother her, wherever she was.

Epilogue

As fate would have it, the nominal wealth of most of the individuals profiled in this book faded after their deaths. Yet their legacies endure.

Mary Ellen Pleasant left a large estate worth nearly $300,000 ($8.4 million) when she died, but she had no heirs to bequeath her fortune to. Her only daughter, Lizzie J. Smith, died when she was a young woman in San Francisco, years before her mother. Pleasant's estate was consumed by her numerous creditors and complainants after she died in 1904.

Robert Reed Church left hundreds of his residential properties in the Beale Street District of Memphis to the children of his first marriage, Mary Church Terrell and Thomas Ayers Church. At the time of their inheritance, the values of these properties were declining, due in part to Beale Street itself, which was once again being maligned as a black slum and vice district. Mary and Thomas thrived despite their diminished inheritance. Mary became a teacher and a prominent suffragette and civil rights activist. Thomas became a lawyer and publisher.

Robert Reed Church left the bulk of his liquid assets to his second wife, Anna Church, and their children, Annette Church and Robert Reed Church Jr., who used their father's bequest to maintain the family's commercial property business on Beale Street. Church Jr. leased property to clubs and concert halls, as Beale Street became the mecca of blues music, eventually serving as a launching pad for W. C. Handy and B. B. King. In doing so, he was part of establishing the black entertainment industry, which today is responsible for the majority of black America's very richest entrepreneurs, including Oprah Winfrey, Bob Johnson, Sean Combs, Tyler Perry, and Cathy Hughes. Church Jr. died in 1952, leaving one daughter, Sara Roberta Church. When she died in 1995, after a career working as an administrator for the federal government, she was the last known surviving direct descendant of Robert Reed Church Sr.

O. W. Gurley had most of his wealth destroyed in the fires and violence of the Tulsa race riots in 1921. Afterward, he moved to a four-bedroom house in South Los Angeles and opened a small hotel that he operated with his wife, Emma. Gurley was never able to rebuild his wealth to the level it had reached in Tulsa. The couple had no children and left a modest estate to their extended family members.

Hannah Elias disappeared from public life after she moved to Europe. What she did after she expatriated is still a mystery. Nonetheless, her most notable achievement was in helping convert Harlem into a black mecca. Today, Harlem remains one of America's most prominent black neighborhoods.

When Annie Malone died of a stroke in 1954, she left behind a diminished estate worth approximately $100,000 ($906,888), coming after years of expenses from the management fees of her company and an expensive divorce from Aaron Malone. As she had no children, her estate was split between her nieces and nephews.

Many of the industries these men and women pioneered are still relevant today. Real estate, which played a role in the development of the fortunes of almost all the dynamic personalities in this book, is still an outsize component of African American wealth. Since Reconstruction, black people have, on average as a group, invested a larger percentage of their net worth in real estate than any other group. There may be many economic and social reasons for this, but perhaps one in particular is that for African Americans, owning one's land, after toiling tirelessly over it as enslaved farmers and then sharecroppers, is an affirmation of liberation. That being said, the 2008 financial crisis dealt a blow to this economic tradition, as African Americans were disproportionately affected by both the fraudulent lending practices that helped create the crisis and the foreclosures that resulted. Today, the black home ownership rate is around 43 percent, nearly the lowest for African Americans in modern history.

Madam C. J. Walker's and Annie Malone's businesses created the black hair and beauty industry, which today is worth nearly $700 million. Surprisingly, the black hair industry today is not dominated by African American companies, or even any American companies, but rather by foreign firms. South Korean and Chinese companies that manufacture products like wigs, hair extensions, and chemical straighteners dominate the black hair sector. The trend, however, may be reversing, as more black women are choosing to wear their hair "natural," just as Annie Malone advocated more than 130 years ago.

Mary Ellen Pleasant and Jeremiah Hamilton were pioneers as black stock and commodity traders. They paved the way for investors like Robert F. Smith, who today is one of America's most successful investors and is worth nearly $3 billion. African Americans have historically underinvested in the markets, due in no small part to the legacy of Jim Crow–era "black bans" on Wall Street, which early black investors like Jeremiah Hamilton, Mary Ellen Pleasant, and my great-great-uncle John Mott Drew had to circumvent just to get in the game. In recent years, the racial investment gap has been closing. Despite this progress, black investment managers are still underrepresented, with only a little over 1 percent of all assets in the United States being managed by black brokers and firms.

During their lives, Mary Ellen Pleasant, Robert Reed Church, Ottawa W. Gurley, Annie Malone, Hannah Elias, and Madam C. J. Walker were pioneers and inspirations to other African Americans and their allies, while to others they were upenders of a racist social order. Slavery and Jim Crow were not just social atrocities, but also economic institutions meant to create a marginally compensated black labor class. As enslaved African Americans became paid tenant farmers after Emancipation, their wages were garnished by plantation owners. Blacks who managed to own their farms faced constant racial harassment and threats from white supremacist groups. African American inventors were often denied patents or had their intellectual property stolen. The black wealthy class perhaps represented the greatest affront to the racist economic systems of the slave and Jim Crow eras. It is perhaps for this reason that the six individuals in this book faced assassination attempts, mob violence, threats, libel, and slander. Yet they persevered to contribute to their communities and bring about some of America's proudest moments, such as the abolition of slavery, the suffrage of women, and the establishment of some of the country's most important cities and industries. These individuals' lives demonstrate that wealth can be used as a powerful resource for change in the right hands, if people are so willing.

The stories of the first black millionaires in America are the beginning of an epic that is still unfolding—the journey from enslavement to economic and social equality. Their unlikely lives provided a spark for a people just beginning to lift themselves out of bondage and still serve as inspiration for minorities and women as they strive for greater financial empowerment today.

Acknowledgments

I'd like to thank my wife, Aprielle Wills, and my aunt Maria Hewlett Gittens, who have supported me and gotten me through what proved to be a challenging researching and writing process. I'd also like to thank Maria and my mother for their help with our family history, which became part of this book.

I'd like to thank my mentors Samuel Freedman and Howard French. This book was conceived in Samuel Freedman's book seminar at Columbia Journalism School, and Sam has seen me all the way through to the publication. Thank you, Sam, for believing in me as a writer and having my back through this entire process. I'd like to thank Howard for being there for me, championing me at every phase, pushing me to be a better reporter and storyteller, and advocating to our wonderful agent, Gloria Loomis, that she sign me and represent this book. Speaking of, I'd like to thank Gloria and Julia Masnik of Watkins-Loomis, who worked with me patiently to find the right publisher for *Black Fortunes*. Gloria and Julia, you've always had my back, and I really appreciate you. Here's to many more books! I want to thank Tracy Sherrod, Amistad, and HarperCollins for believing in me and believing in this book, and for giving me the opportunity of a lifetime to write these stories.

I'd also like to thank Columbia University for all its support in writing this book. I'd like to shout-out my classmates, especially the members of my books seminar, who workshopped an early version of *Black Fortunes*. I also take this space to remember Kim Wall, our classmate who died this year while reporting. I'd also like to thank the Linton family, whose fellowship helped make this book possible.

I'd like to thank the Chatham-Kent Black Historical Society for helping me with my research on Mary Ellen Pleasant and the Chatham Vigilance Committee. I'd like to acknowledge all the other researchers who have worked to unearth these hidden figures. I'd also like to thank the University of Memphis for access to its wonderful online archives. And I'd like to thank the San Francisco Public Library archives for giving me access to the Mary Ellen Pleasant archive.

I want to thank my daughter, Zora, for always keeping me hopeful and motivated and giving me a reason to smile every day. I'd like to thank my friends, who have been there for me through this process: John and Brenda Strickland, Brett Shere, Anthony Walker, Magogodi Makhene, James Clarke, Eddie and Teak Senior,

Alice Sutcliffe and Russell Clinton, Paula Marcet, Tony Speranza, Jonathan Lindsay, and Bergen Cooper. I'd like to thank my in-laws, Duck, Jim, Rain, and Alanna. I'd like to thank my former colleagues Jeffrey Toobin and Caleb Silver from CNN for having my back even after I left, and for all their help with this book. I'd also like to thank Jelani Cobb and Harry Belafonte for taking an interest in me and helping me along the way where they could.

I'd like to thank my father, Reginald Wills, for introducing me to black history and always underscoring its importance. I'd like to thank my sister, Nayo Wills, for her encouragement, and my brother. I'd like to acknowledge my mother, Pamela Hewlett Wills, who passed on to me her writerly sensibilities and championed me more times than I can count. Thank you.

Source Notes

CHAPTER 1

The information about Frederick Douglass's time in Nantucket and his quotations come from his 1855 autobiography, *My Bondage and My Freedom*. The account of his speech comes from correspondence in *The Anti-Slavery Standard* on August 26, 1841. Sheldon Foner's *Frederick Douglass: A Biography* was the source of the information about Douglass's time on Nantucket and his interactions with black Nantucketers.

The biographical information and quotations from Mary Ellen Pleasant come from her two short biographies that she dictated to the journalist Sam P. Davis and which appeared in a periodical called *Pandex of the Press* in 1902 and 1904, titled "Memoirs and Autobiography" and "How a Colored Woman Aided John Brown," respectively. I also used archival material from the San Francisco Library and Pleasant's recipe books, which contain a few personal notes. I leaned heavily on the work of the investigative journalist and Mary Ellen Pleasant researcher Lerone Bennett.

I'd like to address for a moment the belief that Pleasant was an escaped slave from Virginia, a madame, a seductress, or a Voodoo priestess, as popularized by the racist yellow journalism of her day and the specious claims of her ex-employee Charlotte Dennis Downs in Helen Holdredge's 1953 biography *Mammy Pleasant.* Downs claimed that she was Pleasant's secret memoirist, but, when asked to produce evidence, said she had lost the manuscript that Pleasant had dictated to her. I consider the stories stemming from such accounts to be apocryphal. As interesting as they may be, they contradict historical records and Pleasant's multiple documented tellings of her own life story.

I also referenced Lynn Hudson's excellent Mary Ellen Pleasant biography, *The Making of "Mammy Pleasant."* Hudson gives an expansive survey of the known material on Pleasant, including the Holdredge biography, while wading through the innuendo and historical rumor to give a balanced portrait of Pleasant.

CHAPTER 2

My primary source materials for Robert Reed Church were the two biographies published by his relatives, *A Colored Woman in a White World,* by his second daughter, Mary Church Terrell, and *The Robert R. Churches of Memphis: A Father and Son Who Achieved in Spite of Race,* by his daughter and granddaughter Annette and Sara Roberta Church. I also used archival material including his family letters and a family oral history given by Annette and Sara Roberta Church to Memphis State University titled "Robert Church Family of Memphis." Archival letters from the Burton family to the Churches provided a great deal of information on Emmeline's background and history as a slave.

James T. Lloyd's *Steamboat Directory and Disasters on the Western Waters* and Emerson Gould's *Fifty Years on the Mississippi; or, Gould's History of River Navigation* provided additional details on the fire on *Bulletin No. 2.* The quotations in this chapter come from *The Robert R. Churches of Memphis, A Colored Woman in a White World,* the Church family oral history, and the Church family correspondence with the Burton family, who once owned Robert, his brother, and his mother.

CHAPTER 3

The information about Pleasant's arrival and first years in San Francisco comes from her second dictated biography to Sam P. Davis, "How a Colored Woman Aided John Brown," as well as a passenger log from the SS *Oregon,* the ship Pleasant arrived on, published in the *Alta California* in August 1852. I used *The Age of Gold: The California Gold Rush and the New American Dream* by H. W. Brands and *The Barbary Coast* by Herbert Asbury as my main references and sources of material on gold rush–era San Francisco.

Details and quotations about Pleasant's business dealings come from the research of Lerone Bennett, and Davis's "How a Colored Woman Aided Jim Brown."

I excerpted James McCune Smith's essay series on wealth from *The Works of James McCune Smith: Black Intellectual and Abolitionist*, edited by John Staffer, and I obtained biographical information from Shane White's Jeremiah Hamilton biography, *Prince of Darkness*.

The information and quotation on Pleasant's decision to go to Canada, her journey there, and her residence in Chatham come from Sam P. Davis's "How a Colored Woman Aided John Brown." The Chatham-Kent Black Historical Society and Jane Rhodes's *Mary Ann Shadd Cary: The Black Press and Protest in the Nineteenth Century* were invaluable in providing background on blacks and Chatham. I obtained information about the Chatham Vigilance Committee's train robbery from the reporting and court records on the incident, for which I referenced *Race on Trial: Black Defendants in Ontario's Criminal Courts, 1858–1958* by Barrington Walker and *The Black Abolitionist Papers, Volume II: Canada, 1830–1865*, edited by C. Peter Ripley. The information about the Chatham constitutional convention comes from John Brown's letters and essays in *John Brown, Liberator of Kansas and Martyr of Virginia, Life and Letters*, edited by Franklin Benjamin Sanborn.

CHAPTER 4

The information and dialogue contained in this chapter on Robert R. Church's time on the river before and after the Civil War comes from *The Robert R. Churches of Memphis*. My source for material on his first wife and daughter, Margaret and Laura Pico, comes from court records and reporting when Laura Pico sued the Church family in the case of *Napier v. Church*, which I found in *Reports of Cases Argued and Determined in the Supreme Court of Tennessee, Volume 132*. My reporting on the battle of Memphis is based on the battle summary from the Civil War Sites Advisory Commission.

CHAPTER 5

Shane White's account of Jeremiah Hamilton's near lynching in his excellent biography *Prince of Darkness* is impeccably reported and invaluable. I directly referenced the newspaper accounts of the event compiled by Iver Bernstein in *The New York City Draft Riots: Their Significance for American Society and Politics in the Age of Civil War*.

CHAPTER 6

My retelling of Oklahoma's history with slavery and the Confederacy was informed by *Oklahoma, a History of Five Centuries* by Arrell Morgan Gibson, *General Stand Watie's Confederate Indians* by Frank Cunningham, and *Black Slaves, Indian Masters: Slavery, Emancipation, and Citizenship in the Native American South* by Barbara Krauthamer.

CHAPTER 7

The information and quoted material on Church's re-emergence in Memphis, including his marriage to Louisa Ayers, his relationship with his father, the birth of his daughter, and the starting of his first business, comes from *A Colored Woman in a White World*. The saga with

Margaret and Laura Pico again draws on the case files and reporting of *Napier v. Church.*

Beale Street Dynasty: Sex, Song, and the Struggle for the Soul of Memphis by Preston Lauterbach was incredibly informative on Church's billiard-hall-related arrest, Church's experience in the riots, his rebuilding afterward, and his experiences during the yellow fever outbreak. The reporting on the riot and its aftermath draws from the report generated by the United States Congress House Select Committee on the Memphis Riots.

CHAPTER 8

Pleasant's time with the Woodworths was established by the census record that shows her and JJ living at their house. The biographical details on Selim Woodworth come from *The Beginnings of San Francisco* by Zoeth Skinner Eldredge and his obituary printed in *Daily Alta California* on February 2, 1871. Details about the Pleasant Omnibus case comes from a front-page story on the incident in the *Daily Alta California* printed on October 17, 1866.

Details on the second case, against NBMRR, come from the court documents in the case of *John J. Pleasants and Mary E. Pleasants v. NBMRR.*

The information on Pleasant's boardinghouse comes from "How a Colored Woman Aided John Brown." The material on Pleasant's laundry business comes from an account by James Allen Francis Jr., an employee at one of the laundries she owned, listed among the Pleasant archive in the San Francisco Public Library.

The information on Pleasant's mansion and her relationship with and investments in Nevada mining stock comes from the underappreciated investigative journalism of Lerone Bennett published in *Ebony* as "An Historical Detective Story: The Mystery of Mary Ellen Pleasant, Part I" in 1979. It constitutes some of the best research on Mary Ellen Pleasant.

CHAPTER 9

Newspaper reporting on the fire in Memphis from the *Daily Memphis Avalanche* and the *Memphis Daily Appeal* was invaluable in writing about the fire at Church's saloon, as was the account in *Beale Street Dynasty*.

Information about Bob's brother James Wilson comes from *The Robert R. Churches of Memphis* and *A Colored Woman in a White World*. The family oral history "Robert Church Family of Memphis" was the source of the details about Bob and Anna's marriage and home life.

The quotation from and background information on Ida B. Wells in Memphis comes from her letters and diaries, collected nicely in *The Light of the Truth: Writings of an Anti-Lynching Crusader*, edited by Mia Bay.

CHAPTER 10

My background information on the 1893 Oklahoma land run comes from the Oklahoma Historical Society and *Oklahoma, a History of Five Centuries*.

Biographical information on O. W. Gurley's family and early life comes from census records and a 1914 profile of Gurley in the *Tulsa Star*. Information on the town of Perry comes from the Oklahoma Historical Society.

The information on Edward P. McCabe comes from his entry in the *Encyclopedia of African American History, 1896 to the Present,* edited by Paul Finkelman; an article called "Black in Oklahoma" from a *New York Times* correspondent printed in 1891; and *The Story of Oklahoma* by W. David Baird.

<h3 style="text-align:center">CHAPTER 11</h3>

The information about Annie Malone's early life comes from her typed biography, contained in her file in the Claude A. Barnett papers at the Chicago History Museum Research Center, as well as census records that confirm her date of birth, the names of her parents, and the places of her residence. The quotations are taken from a retelling of her life story in a promotional pamphlet printed by Poro in 1925, which is also contained in the Barnett papers. For information on Madam C. J. Walker, I relied on A'Lelia Bundles's comprehensive biography, *On Her Own Ground.*

<h3 style="text-align:center">CHAPTER 12</h3>

The information about Philadelphia's Seventh Ward comes from W. E. B. Du Bois's study of the area in *The Philadelphia Negro.* I sourced Elias's story by compiling the many newspaper articles written about her in the *New York World* and the *New York Times*, both of which covered her scandal and trial and wrote dozens of articles about her after she became a public figure.

The stories of her early life, family, relationship with Frank P. Satterfield, and first and second jailing come from an article called "Rich Elias Once in the Poorhouse" from the *New York Evening World* on November 21, 1903. The story of Platt's meeting Elias in the Tenderloin and the development of their affair comes from an interview he gave after he filed suit against her in the *Evening World* on June 1, 1904. An article in the *Evening World* on November 17, 1903, provides details of Elias's initial questioning as well as information on the birth and death of her daughter, Gwendolyn.

Details about her mansion and home life come from an exposé by one her employees, published by the *Evening World* on June 2, 1904.

CHAPTER 13

Information on Pleasant's ranch comes from the Beltane ranch, which is still in operation. The story of Newton Booth's funeral comes from *The Making of "Mammy Pleasant."*

The accounts of Thomas Bell's death come from the *San Francisco Examiner* on October 16, 1892, and the *San Francisco Chronicle* on October 17, 1892. I also relied on Lerone Bennett's "An Historical Detective Story."

Records on Bell's wealth were destroyed, according to the Mary Ellen Pleasant collection at the San Francisco Public Library. Newspaper sources were used, including a report on Bell's income in the *San Francisco Examiner* on September 9, 1897. Pleasant's wish to be left out of the will comes from J. Lloyd Conrich, "Mammy Pleasant Legend."

Details and quotes from Fred Bell's legal battle with Pleasant come from the *San Francisco Call's* reports on September 9, 10, 16, and 23, 1897, and the *San Francisco Chronicle* on September 10, 15, and 23, 1897. Details about Pleasant's last days and death come from her "Biography and Memoirs" and the reporting of her death in the *San Francisco Examiner* on January 12, 1904, and the *San Francisco Chronicle* on the same date.

CHAPTER 14

Accounts of Church's construction of Church Park come from the archive at Memphis State University and *The Robert R. Churches of Memphis.* The information on Church's relationship with Booker T. Washington comes from the oral history "Robert Church Family of Memphis," as does the information about Church's political activity and his relationship with Roosevelt. The story of Church firing at white harassers during a snowstorm comes from *A Colored Woman in a White World.* The stories about Solvent Savings Bank come from *The Robert R. Churches of Memphis* and the Church family oral history. The stories about Church's death also come from the Church family oral history.

CHAPTER 15

The stories about J. B. Stradford's and O. W. Gurley's development of Greenwood come from a profile written about them in the *Tulsa Star* in 1914 and two excellent Greenwood books, *Riot and Remembrance* by James S. Hirsch and *The Burning* by Tim Madigan.

Reporting on Gurley's early wealth comes from a July 24, 1917, report by the *Muskogee Scimitar*. The story of Stradford's beating of a white man comes from *Hidden History of Tulsa* by Steve Gerkin. The story of O. W. Gurley's fight with three white men comes from a November 11, 1916, report by the *Tulsa Star* on the incident.

CHAPTER 16

The stories and quotes in this chapter come from Annie's biography in the Claude A. Barnett papers and *On Her Own Ground*. Information on Booker T. Washington's death comes from his obituary published in the *New York Times* on November 15, 1915.

CHAPTER 17

An article by the *New York Times* published on November 13, 1903, contains details of Andrew Green's funeral arrangements, the jailing and arraignment of his killer, Cornelius Williams, Williams's confessions, eyewitness accounts of the murder scene, and a few details about Elias and Williams's meeting and Elias's early response to the murder.

A *New York Times* article from June 2, 1904, provides details of Green's suit against Elias for the

$685,000 he gave her, the first attempt at arresting Elias being thwarted by her lawyer, and a full statement by Platt giving the entire story of his relationship with Elias. Another article, on June 4 by the *New York Times*, describes the angry crowd gathering outside her house.

An article in the *Bisbee Daily Review* on June 14, 1904, details her time in prison after she was arrested during the Platt scandal. The story of Elias's day in court, her acquittal, and her return home comes from an article in the *New York Times* on June 11, 1904. The same article includes the transcripts of the court testimony and an interview with Elias after the acquittal which are used in the chapter.

CHAPTER 18

Information on the nineteenth annual National Negro Business League comes from *The Negro Year Book: An Annual Encyclopedia of the Negro, 1937–1938*. Information on Annie and C. J. Walker comes from the Annie Malone papers in the Claude A. Barnett collection and *On Her Own Ground*.

CHAPTER 19

The stories of the Tulsa riots come from *Riot and Remembrance* and *The Burning*. Information on Gurley's life after the riots and his financial losses comes from the Greenwood Historical Center.

CHAPTER 20

The story of the evictions of whites in Harlem comes from an article entitled "Hannah Elias Evicts White Tenants" in the *New York Evening World* on July 9, 1906. *Harlem: The Four-Hundred-Year History from Dutch Village to Capital of Black America* by Jonathan Gill was an essential reference in writing about the development of Harlem. The story of another eviction of whites by Elias comes from the *New York Tribune* on November 11, 1905. The report of her expatriation comes from the *New York Evening World* in 1921.

Index

About the Author

SHOMARI WILLS is a journalist. He has worked for CNN and *Good Morning America*, and has contributed to *New York Carib News* and *Columbia Journalism Review*. He received an undergraduate degree from Morehouse College and a graduate degree from Columbia University, where he was named a Lynton Book Writing Fellow. He lives in Brooklyn, New York.